A New Owner's
GUIDE TO
GREAT DANES

JG-115

Opposite page: Homewood Country Sunshine and puppy Ch. Sunnyside Daffodil owned by Jill Swedlow.

The Publisher wishes to acknowledge the following owners of the dogs in this book: Rick and Judy Abrams, Marnie Baker, Diana Bartlett, BMW Harlequins, Dorothy Carlson, the Dillon family, Richard E. and Jane B. Farmer, Joan Fonfa, Vicki Gardner, Laura Kiaulenas, Paddy Magnuson, Brucie Mitchell, Billy Moriera, Lois Ostrowski, Chris Salyers, Kandi Sterling, Rosalie Strawcutter, Kathy and Mike Strouse, Jill Swedlow, Willowdane Kennels, Betty Wilson.

Photographers: Michael Allen, Rich Bergman, Wayne Cott, Wendy Dillon, Isabelle Francais, Vicki Gardner, Robert Pearcy, Vince Serbin, Jill Swedlow, Missy Yuhl.

The author acknowledges the contribution of Judy Iby of the following chapters: Sport of Purebred Dogs, Identification and Finding the Lost Dog, Traveling with Your Dog, Health Care, Behavior and Canine Communication.

Distributed in the UNITED STATES to the Pet Trade by T.F.H. Publications, Inc., One T.F.H. Plaza, Neptune City, NJ 07753; distributed in the UNITED STATES to the Bookstore and Library Trade by National Book Network, Inc. 4720 Boston Way, Lanham MD 20706; in CANADA to the Pet Trade by H & L Pet Supplies Inc., 27 Kingston Crescent, Kitchener, Ontario N2B 2T6; Rolf C. Hagen Inc., 3225 Sartelon St. Laurent-Montreal Quebec H4R 1E8; in CANADA to the Book Trade by Vanwell Publishing Ltd., 1 Northrup Crescent, St. Catharines, Ontario L2M 6P5 ; in ENGLAND by T.F.H. Publications, PO Box 15, Waterlooville PO7 6BQ; in AUSTRALIA AND THE SOUTH PACIFIC by T.F.H. (Australia), Pty. Ltd., Box 149, Brookvale 2100 N.S.W., Australia; in NEW ZEALAND by Brooklands Aquarium Ltd. 5 McGiven Drive, New Plymouth, RD1 New Zealand; in Japan by T.F.H. Publications, Japan—Jiro Tsuda, 10-12-3 Ohjidai, Sakura, Chiba 285, Japan; in SOUTH AFRICA by Lopis (Pty) Ltd., P.O. Box 39127, Booysens, 2016, Johannesburg, South Africa. Published by T.F.H. Publications, Inc.
MANUFACTURED IN THE
UNITED STATES OF AMERICA
BY T.F.H. PUBLICATIONS, INC.

A NEW OWNER'S
GUIDE TO
GREAT DANES

JILL SWEDLOW

Contents

1997 Edition

A quartet of adorable Great Dane puppies.

Living with a dog the size of a Great Dane presents many challenges.

A Great Dane is a loving, welcomed addition to any family.

These Great Danes exemplify the dignified and majestic presence the breed possesses.

The versatile Great Dane excels at everything from conformation to therapy work.

HISTORY of the Great Dane

There is not much disagreement that the breed known today as the Great Dane has ancient origins. For example, there is a Grecian coin in the Royal Museum at Munich that dates from the fifth century BC, and it depicts a likeness of a dog that greatly resembles the modern Great Dane. Pictures that closely resemble the Dane have appeared on artifacts of many ancient civilizations. Pre-biblical Assyria, Egypt, ancient Greece and Rome all have artistic evidence of Dane-like dogs.

The earliest of these dogs were called "Bullenbeissers" and were very similar to the breed we call the Mastiff. The Mastiff, as we know it today, was developed in England, but the Bullenbeisser was definitely of early Germanic origins and was the basic dog from which the many Mastiff-type dogs have emerged. From the earliest times, a strain of dogs of the Bullenbeisser type has played a dramatic part in the history of mankind. The ancient Assyrians used these massive,

The earliest Dane-like dog was a hunting dog who used his strength and agility to bring down wild boars.

courageous, fierce animals as war and guard dogs, and they were eventually called "molossis" or Molossian dogs after the ancient Grecian city.

These huge dogs were known in ancient Egypt and conquering Rome and were in common use among the early Tuetonic and Celtic tribes. Crude drawings and literary references show that through the Middle Ages the large Bullenbeisser was the most commonly used guard dog in Germany, where it was known as the "Deutsche Dogge," or German dog. Bullenbeissers were also originally hunting dogs,

It is believed that the Great Dane's ancestors were warriors and guardians, and served as weapons during ancient battles. used to chase and bring down mainly wild boars, but also cattle, wolves and elk. Their ears were cropped extremely short to prevent injury as the dog ran through heavy brush and to prevent damage inflicted by the sharp tusks of the boar. As time passed, the wild boar became scarce and "boarhounds," as they were also called, were not needed anymore.

Few people are aware that Dane-like dogs were extensively used as offensive weapons as well, before the invention of gunpowder. The Gauls developed armor with jointed plates of metal and light chain for the early ancestors of the Great Dane. Attila the Hun utilized these types of dogs to guard his camps from surprise enemy attacks, and Charles V of Spain used more than 400 dogs, sent to him from England by Henry VIII, in his battle against Francis I. Meanwhile, in the British Isles, animals of the same root stock were fashioned into the English Mastiff, and, through crossings with Greyhounds and Irish Wolf-hounds, the basic Bullenbeisser breed pattern was altered and refined and a breed was developed that was to eventually become the Great Dane.

The development of the modern pure-bred Great Dane began about the middle of the 19th century, along with the advent of competitive dog shows in England and in the rest of Europe. The breed grew enormously and, in 1887, the Stuttgart show in Germany had an entry of 300 Great Danes. The world's first Great Dane Club was formed in England in about 1883, and the German Duetsche-Doggen Club was formed in 1888. The Duetsche-Doggen Club must be given credit for selectively breeding towards the ideal Dane. At the time, the dogs in northern Germany had been aggressive,

Thanks to the efforts of responsible and selective breeders, the Great Dane's temperament and reputation have greatly improved over the years.

The Great Dane as we know it today emerged in the 19th century. Sunnyside Jonquilla is a modern example of the breed.

heavy and coarse, while the southern Dane was more mild, slender and elegant-looking. The members of the club set the standard between the two types and began keeping detailed records of pedigrees, prize winners and breeding practices. A preliminary standard had been drawn up in Germany in 1800, but both the American and British standards, the official descriptions of the ideal specimen, are based upon quite literal translations of the German standard adopted by the Duetsche-Doggen Club in 1891. Club member Edward Messter of Nill is an important pioneer because his brindle Dane, Nero I 609, is considered the principal progenitor of all modern Great Danes. This is because nearly all Dane pedigrees of all colors eventually lead back to him at some point.

In 1857, the first Great Dane was imported into the United States by Mr. Francis Butler. This was a harlequin Dane named Prince who was imported from London. The first time Great Danes were shown in America was in 1877 at the Philadelphia

Grand National Show. They were then shown under the name
of Siberian or Elm dogs. Finally, in 1886, for the first time in
this country, a Great Dane was entered and shown under the
classification "Great Dane." The dog, a brindle male named
Tiger, was owned by Mr. J. Blackburn Miller. The Great Dane
Club of America was formed in 1889, and is still a guide and
inspiration in the Great Dane fancy today.

The temperament of these early Danes, imported directly
from Germany, was so aggressive as to be almost
unmanageable. Their use as hunting dogs by day and guard
dogs by night required this type of temperament, but they
were considered so bad that they were banned from dog
shows in the U.S. for several years. The tremendous
improvement in temperament within about 20 years of the first
imports can be attributed to the early American breeders. One
of the most important breakthroughs in the early evolution of
the breed was the first Great Dane Club specialty show held on
Long Island, New York. Helios von Wurtemburg, owned by
Mr. John Buck of Omaha, Nebraska, placed first out of 80
entered Danes. During the early 1900s, the Great Dane's
popularity soared in America. From 1920 to 1935, a total of
163 Great Danes won the title of champion and only 78 were
imported from other countries.

But after World War I, the breed was waning in Europe due
to conditions such as food shortages and rabies scares. A great
effort was undertaken to revitalize the breed. Purebred Danes
were rescued from homelessness and hunger and if accepted
by a panel of judges, were deemed foundlings and placed
under conditional registration. Despite obvious hardships in
Germany, this was a defining time for the Great Dane. A family
of nearly perfect Great Danes arrived at the von der Saalburg
kennels of Karl Farber in Bad Homburg. The mating of the

*Great Danes
come in a variety
of colors, each
having a charm
all its own. These
black puppies are
hard to resist!*

brindle bitch Fauna Moguntia to golden-fawn Ch. Bosko vd Saalburg in 1924 produced the brindle Ch. Dolf vd Saalburg. The legacy of these important Danes is immeasurable and has set the type in all colors to the present day.

Caring and responsible breeders, preserving the breed's integrity, have retained the Great Dane's enormous capacity for devotion and loyalty, and allowed for the "Apollo of Dogs" to evolve into the most gentle of giants.

These gray and black harlequin puppies are examples of the interesting coat coloration that can emerge in the Great Dane.

Known as the "Apollo of Dogs," the Great Dane has proved to be a loyal and devoted companion. Author Jill Swedlow poses with her friend Ch. Sunnyside Cricket.

STANDARD for the Great Dane

Breed standards are like a blueprint. They describe the ideal for the breed to which they apply. It is the dog described in the standard that the breeder must strive to produce. Until this concept is fully understood, a person should refrain from breeding. There will never be a "perfect" dog of any breed. Even the Best in Show dogs within a breed are not perfect, although they probably have fewer faults than most. A novice can and should read the standard of the breed prior to selecting his or her Great Dane, although it is a rare novice who will fully understand it exactly. The complete standard, as approved by the American Kennel Club, appears below. Read and study it. If you can, take a knowledgeable friend with you when interviewing breeders and looking at litters.

THE OFFICIAL STANDARD OF THE GREAT DANE

General Appearance–The Great Dane combines, in its regal appearance, dignity, strength and elegance with great size and a powerful, well-formed, smoothly muscled body. It is one of the giant working breeds, but is unique in that its general conformation must be so well balanced that it never appears clumsy, and shall move with a long reach and powerful drive. It is always a unit– the Apollo of dogs. A Great Dane must be spirited, courageous, never timid; always friendly and dependable. This physical and mental combination is the characteristic which gives the Great Dane the majesty possessed by no other breed. It is particularly true of this breed that there is an impression of great masculinity in dogs, as

The Great Dane is a giant, working breed whose massive presence suggests his power, spirit and elegance.

Despite his awesome size, the Great Dane carries himself with a great deal of grace and balance.

compared to an impression of femininity in bitches. Lack of true Dane breed type, as defined in this standard, is a serious fault.

Size, Proportion, Substance—The male should appear more massive throughout than the bitch, with larger frame and heavier bone. In the ratio between length and height, the Great Dane should be square. In bitches, a somewhat longer body is permissible, providing she is well proportioned to her height. Coarseness or lack of substance are equally undesirable. The male shall not be less than 30 inches at the shoulders, but it is preferable that he be 32 inches or more, providing he is well proportioned to his height. The female shall not be less than 28 inches at the shoulders, but it is preferable that she be 30 inches or more, providing she is well proportioned to her height. Danes under minimum height must be disqualified.

Head—The head shall be rectangular, long, distinguished, expressive, finely chiseled, especially below the eyes. Seen from the side, the Dane's forehead must be sharply set off from the bridge of the nose, (a strongly pronounced stop). The plane of

A Great Dane possesses chiseled features and a long, rectangular head that is proportionate to the rest of his body. If cropped, the ears should be proportionate to the head and carried erect.

the skull and the plane of the muzzle must be straight and parallel to one another. The skull plane under and to the inner point of the eye must slope without any bony protuberance in a smooth line to a full square jaw with a deep muzzle (fluttering lips are undesirable). The masculinity of the male is very pronounced in structural appearance of the head. The bitch's head is more delicately formed. Seen from the top, the skull should have parallel sides and the bridge of the nose should be as broad as possible. The cheek muscles should not be prominent. The length from the tip of the nose to the center of the stop should be equal to the length from the center of the stop to the rear of the slightly developed occiput. The head should be angular from all sides and should have flat planes with dimensions in proportion to the size of the Dane. Whiskers may be trimmed or left natural.

Eyes shall be medium size, deep set, and dark, with a lively intelligent expression. The eyelids are almond-shaped and relatively tight, with well developed brows. Haws and Mongolian eyes are serious faults. In harlequins, the eyes should be dark; light colored eyes, eyes of different colors and walleyes are permitted but not desirable.

Your Dane's eyes should be dark, deep-set and lively and should convey intelligence. Eyes of lighter colors are acceptable, but not desirable.

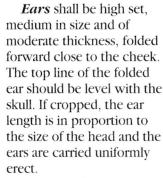

Ears shall be high set, medium in size and of moderate thickness, folded forward close to the cheek. The top line of the folded ear should be level with the skull. If cropped, the ear length is in proportion to the size of the head and the ears are carried uniformly erect.

Nose shall be black, except in the blue Dane, where it is a dark blue-black. A black spotted nose is permitted on the harlequin; a pink colored nose is not desirable. A split nose is a disqualification.

Teeth shall be strong, well developed, clean and with full dentition. The incisors of the lower jaw touch very lightly the bottoms of the inner surface of the upper incisors (scissors bite). An undershot jaw is a very serious fault. Overshot or wry bites are serious faults. Even bites, misaligned or crowded incisors are minor faults.

Neck, Topline, Body—The neck shall be firm, high set, well arched, long and muscular. From the nape, it should gradually broaden and flow smoothly into the withers. The neck underline should be clean. Withers shall slope smoothly into a short level back with a broad loin. The chest shall be broad, deep and well muscled. The forechest should be well developed without a pronounced sternum. The brisket extends to the elbow, with well sprung ribs. The body underline should be tightly muscled with a well-defined tuck-up. The croup should be broad and very slightly sloping. The tail should be set high and smoothly into the croup, but not quite level with the back, a continuation of the spine. The tail should be broad at the base, tapering uniformly down to the hock joint. At rest, the tail should fall straight. When excited or running, it may curve slightly, but never above the level of the back. A ring or hooked tail is a serious fault. A docked tail is a disqualification.

Forequarters—The forequarters, viewed from the side, shall be strong and muscular. The shoulder blade must be strong and sloping, forming, as near as possible, a right angle in its articulation with the upper arm. A line from the upper tip of the shoulder to the back of the elbow joint should be perpendicular. The ligaments and muscles holding the shoulder blade to the rib cage must be well developed, firm and securely

A Great Dane puppy is a miniature version of his parents. That is why good breeding is very important to produce quality offspring.

attached to prevent loose shoulders. The shoulder blade and the upper arm should be the same length. The elbow should be one-half the distance from the withers to the ground. The strong pasterns should slope slightly. The feet should be round and compact with well-arched toes, neither toeing in, toeing out, nor rolling to the inside or outside. The nails should be short, strong and as dark as possible, except that they may be lighter in harlequins. Dewclaws may or may not be removed.

Hindquarters–The hindquarters shall be strong, broad, muscular and well angulated, with well let down hocks. Seen from the rear, the hock joints appear to be perfectly straight, turned neither toward the inside nor toward the outside. The rear feet should be round and compact, with well-arched toes, neither toeing in nor out. The nails should be short, strong and as dark as possible, except they may be lighter in harlequins. Wolf claws are a serious fault.

These Danes—one fawn and one brindle—are examples of two of the acceptable coat colors in the Great Dane.

Coat–The coat shall be short, thick and clean with a smooth glossy appearance.

Color, Markings and Patterns–*Brindle*–The base color shall be yellow gold and always brindled with strong black cross stripes in a chevron pattern. A black mask is preferred. Black should appear on the eye rims and eyebrows, and may appear on the ears and tail tip. The more intensive the base color and the more distinct and even the brindling, the more preferred will be the color. Too much or too little brindling are equally undesirable. White markings at the chest and toes, black-fronted, dirty colored brindles are not desirable.

Fawn–The color shall be yellow gold with a black mask. Black should appear on the eye rims and eyebrows, and may appear on the ears and tail tip. The deep yellow gold must always be given the preference. White markings at the chest and toes, black-fronted dirty colored fawns are not desirable.

Blue–The color shall be a pure steel blue. White markings at the chest and toes are not desirable.

Black–The color shall be a glossy black. White markings at the chest and toes are not desirable.

Harlequin–Base color shall be pure white with black torn patches irregularly and well distributed over the entire body; a pure white neck is preferred. The black patches should never be large enough to give the appearance of a blanket, nor so small as to give a stippled or dappled effect. Eligible, but less desirable, are a few small gray patches, or a white base with single black hairs showing through, which tend to give a salt and pepper or dirty effect.

The Great Dane possesses a courageous and regal bearing that, coupled with his protective nature, make him an excellent watchdog and companion.

Any variance in color or markings as described above shall be faulted to the extent of the deviation. Any Great Dane which does not fall within the above color classifications must be disqualified.

Gait–The gait denotes strength and power with long, easy strides resulting in no tossing, rolling or bouncing of the topline or body. The backline shall appear level and parallel to the ground. The long reach should strike the ground below the nose while the head is carried forward. The powerful rear drive should be balanced to the reach. As speed increases, there is a natural tendency for the legs to converge toward the centerline of balance beneath the body. There should be no twisting in or out at the elbow or hock joints.

Temperament–The Great Dane must be spirited, courageous, always friendly and dependable, and never timid or aggressive.

DISQUALIFICATIONS–Danes under minimum height, split nose, docked tail, any color other than those described under "Color, Markings and Patterns."

A Great Dane's power lies not only in his size, but also in his gait. He moves quickly and evenly, with long, easy strides.

CHARACTERISTICS of the Great Dane

Great Danes are not the breed for everyone who thinks that they want one. In many cases, the beauty and size of this dog are its first attractions, but the size can later be the reason people get rid of the dog. It's something I've never understood! When you buy a giant breed, you certainly must be aware that the dog will grow to be a very big animal, indeed! If you're not prepared to have your coffee table emptied of its contents with one swipe of a tail, or your yard turned into a mine field, think twice about buying a Dane.

Living with dogs the size of Great Danes can be challenging. They enjoy being with people and often forget how big they really are!

Before making your final decision on owning a Dane, please, spend some time with breeders, in their house, with at least one or two adult Great Danes. Somehow, they never seem as large outdoors as they do indoors. Ideally the breeder will allow one or two of her adults to join you while you discuss the possibility of becoming a Dane owner. Please be sure you can live with the size before you buy!

GENTLE GIANTS

Living with Great Danes is quite an experience and most of us who have lived with them will never be without one. All of mine have pillow beds upstairs in my bedroom and they all sleep there with me. In the morning they galump down the stairs, eat their breakfast and then usually flop down somewhere for their morning naps. The younger ones will often spend some time outdoors exploring and playing. When they're all in the house, they usually just lie around snoozing

Despite their size, all Danes think they are lap dogs. They are extremely affectionate and love to be cuddled. Poppy is getting plenty of attention from her friend Amy.

unless they hear something worth investigating outdoors. They're easy dogs to have around because they are basically quiet. Youngsters, of course, can get pretty rowdy, but mine are taught that rough-housing takes place outside, not in the living room.

Danes love being with their people and are very cuddly dogs. They love to lean on you, climb in your lap if allowed, and are ecstatic if you take time to pet and love them. (How could you not?) If I look like I'm even thinking of going somewhere in the car, they about knock the door down vying to go with me! However, if I say "no" they know I mean it.

Sweet and wonderful as they are, Great Danes, like all breeds, have their drawbacks. First on the list is their normally short life span. Seven to eight years is probably a high average, although there certainly are exceptions. I've been very fortunate to have most of mine live from nine to twelve years. Mine aren't the only ones who tend to outlive the average and this should be on your list of questions to ask a breeder when looking for your puppy.

Obviously, there must be some causes for their early deaths. Unfortunately it seems as if Great Danes have more than their share of health problems. Although not all the problems listed below are life-threatening, they do seem to occur more frequently in Great Danes. If you're considering adding a Dane to your family, you should be aware of them.

COMMON HEALTH PROBLEMS

Von Willebrand's disease, thyroid imbalance and cataracts are some of the more recent health problems that breeders are beginning to screen for. Chances are they will never be a concern to you, but it doesn't hurt to be aware of them and to ask the breeder you're considering buying from if they screen for them.

Von Willebrand's Disease

Von Willebrand's Disease (vWD), is an inherited disorder that causes the blood to fail to clot. Screening consists of a blood test, which yields differing grades of vWD ranging from clear to genetic carrier to affected.

Thyroid

Thyroid problems consist of either over- or under-active thyroid. Since the thyroid can affect many different aspects of a dog's health, a correct function is important. This, too, is a blood test. The OFA (The Orthopedic Foundation for Animals) now certifies dogs with normal thyroid. Abnormal thyroid can effect skin condition (dry, itchy skin with sparse hair cover), the immune system (autoimmune problems), and the reproductive system (sterility).

Cataracts

There are many causes for cataracts such as injury, congenital, nutrition, and inheritance. It is the inherited problems that mainly concern us here. Juvenile cataracts, or inherited cataracts, have been diagnosed in Great Danes but, unfortunately, not many Danes are screened. Screening is important because cataracts cannot always be seen with the naked eye. They are found on the lens, the clear body behind the iris, or colored part, of the eye. Often a cataract will not be visible until the iris is dilated. Currently there is not sufficient data on this problem in Danes to draw any conclusions. A Dane with a cataract may not live long enough for a cataract to ever bother them.

Eyes must be examined by a certified veterinary ophthalmologist for cataracts. If the dog passes its examination, it is issued a CERF (Canine Eye Registration Foundation) number. This number is good for one year after the date of examination. The number then expires and it is recommended that eyes be examined yearly.

Screen your Dane's eyes for signs of cataracts and have his eyes certified by the Canine Eye Registration Foundation (CERF).

Panosteitis

Of all the problems that beset the Great Dane, if you *must* have one, this is the one to choose. Panosteitis is a self-limiting lameness caused by inflammation in the long bones of the leg. It can move from leg to leg and usually goes away on its own. If pain is severe, a trip to the vet is in order. The cause is unknown. Onset is usually between four and eight months of age, and it is almost always gone by two years of age, with one year being most common.

Hip Dysplasia

This is one problem that is becoming rare in our breed in those lines that are faithfully screened by hip x-ray and OFA (Orthopedic Foundation for Animals). There are still, unfortunately, some breeders who justify not checking hips on their Danes by saying they've never had it. It is these breeders who still have a high incidence of hip dysplasia. If you don't x-ray, you don't know. You cannot tell if a dog is dysplastic by the way it moves. Some of the best movers can have the worst hips and vice versa.

Hip dysplasia occurs when the ends (acetabulae) of the femur bone, which is the long thigh bone that joins the pelvis, does not fit snugly into the socket of the pelvis. This is usually because the socket itself is too shallow to accommodate the acetabulum. Because they do not fit correctly, arthritis often develops, which causes the dog to experience pain.

Bloat or Gastric Torsion

Bloat, or gastric torsion, is probably one of the most common causes of death in Great Danes. Recent studies have shown that approximately 25% of all Great Danes will experience bloat. In most cases, bloat does not occur until the dog is past five years of age. It is still unknown as to what actually causes bloat. The stomach fills with gas but is unable to expel it. As the stomach continues to enlarge, it begins to rotate on its axis, flipping over and, in so doing, occluding the nerves and blood vessels. At this point, tissues that are serviced by these vessels begin to die and give off toxins which, in turn, begin to involve the entire animal, causing toxicity, shock and eventual death. Sometimes, even though you might get your Dane to the vet in time for surgery, he'll go through the surgery and then die of heart failure due to his recent trauma.

Treatment for bloat consists of first stabilizing the dog prior to surgery. Passing a stomach tube will allow the trapped gas to escape and reduce the deadly syndrome. Once the dog is deemed a good surgical risk, the vet will open the dog and fix the stomach so that it cannot ever torsion again. There are

Before purchasing a Great Dane, make sure the breeder has screened parents for hip dysplasia with the Orthopedic Foundation for Animals (OFA).

several methods for this, and you should discuss them with your vet *prior* to any incident of bloat. You should also ask your veterinarian how familiar he is with this surgical procedure. If the stomach is only "tacked," you've wasted your money as the tacking will become ineffective within six months. There are other, permanent methods of treating this problem. However, even though you're preventing a future torsion, another bloat episode is possible.

Danes are prone to bloat, so you must monitor what they eat and drink very carefully. These Dane pups are enjoying their first taste of snow.

I have begun to have a gastropexy performed on all my bitches when they are spayed. I have friends who say they do this on their males at the time of hip x-ray (probably because most vets will use anesthetic to do the hip x-ray). With the likelihood of bloat so high, the peace of mind is worth it to me.

Hypertrophic Osteodystrophy (HOD)

Hypertrophic osteodystrophy (HOD) is a disease that affects youngsters, usually from around four months to ten months, during the fastest period of growth. It causes great pain and swelling and inflammation in the joints, sometimes so severe that the dog just lies there and cries. It is diagnosed via x-ray and there are several methods of treatment, pain control being one of the most important. The cause is still unknown and many vets don't even recognize it when it's presented. If caught early, treatment is usually successful.

Wobblers Syndrome

Wobblers Syndrome is a disease of the nervous system that causes the dog to have problems with movement. There are several degrees of this problem. Some dogs can live long lives with it, and some must be euthanized at a young age. It is caused by abnormally formed vertebra in the neck, causing pressure on the spinal cord. The first symptom is often a loss of coordination (ataxia) of the movement of the hind limbs. The dog moves as if it doesn't know exactly where its hind legs are, in extreme cases even falling when making a turn. In severe cases the front limbs may also become involved. Rarely is there pain involved with Wobblers Syndrome and many affected dogs live long normal lives.

Cardiomyopathy

Cardiomyopathy is common in the breed. Most heart problems do not affect the dog until he is three to four years or older. You might notice intermittent coughing, lack of energy, lack of interest in food or exercise intolerance. Sometimes fluids will collect in the stomach and chest cavity or you might notice swelling in the legs. Once diagnosed, cardiomyopathy patients usually only have about three months at best.

Cancer (Osteosarcoma)

Osteosarcoma is the most common form of cancer found in Great Danes. It usually will affect one of the long bones of the leg. You might notice a swelling and/or limping at first. An x-ray is the usual form of diagnosis. If caught prior to metastasis (spreading), amputation of the affected limb may prolong life. Many Danes do very well with amputation and run and play as if they still had their leg. Of course, the age and soundness of your dog will be a major factor in this decision. Those who have opted for amputation say they would do it again in a heartbeat!

Because our Danes have so many potential health problems, conscientious breeders will screen their breeding stock prior to making breeding decisions. The OFA (Orthopedic Foundation for Animals) evaluates hip x-rays and issues a certificate stating the grade of hip—poor, good, or excellent. The owner of the dog will also be advised if the dog is found to be dysplastic. The OFA now also evaluates and registers dogs for thyroid function, elbow dysplasia, and heart defects.

Eyes are certified by CERF (Canine Eye Registration Foundation) after the dog is examined by a Board Certified Canine Ophthalmologist.

OTHER DANE-GERS

Most people don't realize that Great Danes must grow in one year the same amount as humans do in eighteen years! If anything small goes wrong with the metabolism or assimilation of nutrients during this very sensitive period, it's going to show up in the skeleton. Many of these problems can be managed or prevented with proper nutrition: a diet that includes all the elements for growth in the proper balance but effectively slows the growth rate. Keep in mind that although all the above problems are daunting, there is no reason your future Dane cannot live out a long life free from any of them. Owning a Great Dane does not always mean problems!

Aside from health problems, a teething Dane puppy can do a lot of damage in a short time. You must be prepared to prevent this kind of damage and prepared to laugh it off if the dog eats your new sofa. It *does* happen! It helps if you always have plenty of Nylabones® on hand for your Great Dane puppy to chew. If you are the kind of person who must have a home with everything in its place and immaculate at all times, a Great Dane is not your breed.

Heidi poses with six-year-old Heather and five-month-old Matthew Dillon. Matthew and Heidi are the same age, which demonstrates just how fast Danes grow.

However, if you think it would be amusing to have a full grown Dane plant his rear end in your lap (because all Danes think they're lap dogs); if you would be inclined to laugh instead of cry when the dog removed the evening dinner from the counter top; if you would not go into cardiac arrest if you found your best shoes in shreds, then you're the kind of person who would enjoy life with a Great Dane.

The teething period begins at the time the first baby teeth appear at around 12 days and ends with the full development of the adult teeth at about 10 months. The hardest time for your Great Dane puppy is between three and four months, when the deciduous teeth fall out and the adult teeth come in. It can even affect his newly cropped ears. Your puppy will want to chew on anything during this time. Make sure he has a lot of Nylabones® to chew on.

Your all-muscle Great Dane needs a chew device that's up to his standards, and with the Hercules™ bone, he's got one. The unique design of the Hercules™ enables aggressive chewers to grab on to it anywhere for a solid, satisfying chew. Angled like the mighty arm of the mythical strong man himself, the Hercules™ won't give up before your Dane does. Plus it's got raised dental tips that help fight plaque on your chow-hound's chops. Available at your local pet shop.

Danes are fun-loving, curious dogs and will get into just about anything. Grandma Amber tolerates the rowdy attentions of her granddaughter, Cricket.

This will keep your Dane away from things he shouldn't chew on—like your furniture.

Great Danes can be very mischievous. One of mine became proficient at opening just about anything. Eventually I had to keep bungie cords on the refrigerator or she'd clean it out when I wasn't around to stop her. I also had baby locks on all the cupboards that contained food and the trash can cupboard, as she was good at opening those too! Frankly, I thought it was funny, but some wouldn't.

You'll probably never need to worry about intruders with Danes around. Their size alone and the deep bark is usually enough to discourage any would-be thief. And if you're ever truly threatened, you couldn't want a better protector! Even the most mild-mannered Danes can surprise their owners. I've heard stories of Dane owners being shocked at the sudden protectiveness of their dog when they were in a scary situation.

If, after having read the above, you *still* want a Great Dane, then by all means, get one. You'll never regret it!

SELECTING Your Great Dane

WHERE DO YOU GET A DANE?

Whether you're going to buy a show dog or a resident couch potato/companion, you want to be assured that you're acquiring your new "child" from a reputable source who will stand behind its dogs. It isn't likely that you'll find this in a newspaper ad or on the bulletin board at the local supermarket. You should begin your search at the local dog show.

How do you locate the shows? There are several ways. Perhaps one of the best investments would be a subscription to the *AKC Gazette*, the official publication of the American Kennel Club. You can reach them at 51 Madison Avenue, New York, NY 10010. Along with the monthly magazine, you will also receive an *Events Calendar* that lists all the shows and trials in the United States for a three-month period. By contacting the dog show superintendent responsible for a certain show, you can find out how to get to the show grounds and what time Great Danes will be shown. Some local newspapers list upcoming shows, and *Dog World* magazine also has a rather comprehensive list of shows around the country.

If you are serious about a show dog, then it will be worthwhile to take extra time to decide exactly what you're looking for. A subscription to the *Great Dane Reporter* is the best place to start. You can reach them at PO Box 150, Riverside, CA 92502-0150. In the *Reporter* you will see ads from around the country and photographs of the winning Danes. You will begin to get a feel for what "styles" you like within the breed and whose lines appeal to you most. You will probably be able to see many of these dogs at a local show or two. You can decide if you like the dogs in person as much as you did in the pictures. As you become more familiar with the different breeders, you'll begin to zero in on where your new puppy will come from. At this point, you should ask to visit the various kennels and begin talking with the breeders you like.

If you're new to the breed you should obtain a copy of the illustrated breed standard for the Great Dane. You may do this through the Great Dane Club of America at 442 Country View Lane, Garland, TX 75043. Read and study it. (GDCA also has an Internet site at :http://www.users.com/king/g/gdca.) Take it with you to the shows and compare the dogs in the ring to it. (That's what the judge is doing!) If you know someone who is knowledgeable in the breed, ask them to help you learn about correct conformation and temperament. Once you have a little background, you'll feel more confident when buying your puppy. If your friend will help you when you evaluate litters, so much the better. However, your best bet in obtaining a good show prospect (as well as a wonderful pet) is to find a breeder who cares about the breed and is concerned about where his or her pups will spend the rest of their lives.

Before selecting your Great Dane puppy, find out as much as possible about him and his parents' medical and genetic background.

ABOUT BREEDERS

Breeders who care more for the welfare of Great Danes than for the

lining of their bank accounts have several traits in common. First, they probably don't breed more than one or, rarely, two litters a year. They always x-ray their dogs for hip dysplasia, will submit the x-rays for OFA certification, and will insist on the same from the stud owner. They may also screen for thyroid function, heart health, cataracts, and von Willebrand's disease. They will put you through the third degree when you come to buy a puppy. You'll be asked why you want a Dane; if you have a fenced yard; if the Dane will be a house dog; if your bank account can handle an emergency surgery; and, most likely, for references. You might even be asked if the breeder can visit your home before they'll sell a puppy to you. You will be required to bring both your spouse and kids (if any) when you come to meet the puppies. Lastly,

Puppies are very vulnerable when first born—they need lots of food, warmth and sleep.

caring breeders will insist on a spay/ neuter contract or a limited registration on puppies sold as pets. In fact, they may even have already neutered the puppy themselves.

Great Dane puppies need to be socialized with people when young in order to become well-adjusted family pets.

If you are new to the breed you will probably be advised of the many health and growth problems that can afflict Great Danes. It is not unreasonable to expect some type of health and temperament guarantee on your new puppy. Most breeders will offer this, but each does it a different way. At the very least you should have a health guarantee for 48 hours, allowing you to take the puppy to a vet for a general check-up. Few breeders will allow a puppy to go to its new home prior to the age of eight weeks, and many will not allow a puppy to go until its ears have been cropped, at around nine to ten weeks of age. Avoid a breeder who releases a puppy before the age of seven weeks!

By the time your puppy is ready to go home with you, he should have had at least one parvo vaccine (preferably two) and have been checked for intestinal parasites and treated accordingly. Since most pups are going to be at least eight weeks old, they'll probably also have had their first DHLP vaccine. All these records, with the products used, should be given to you by the breeder along with a pedigree, the blue slip (AKC registration application) and the health guarantee in writing.

Breeders who care about their puppies will insist that you contact them if you should ever need to place your dog, no matter what age. Most will buy the dog back or help place him in an appropriate home. For those who care, it's heart wrenching to find they've lost track of one of their puppies.

Conscientious breeders also make it known to all puppy buyers that they are not only free to, but should contact them if they have any questions, no matter how trivial. It's sort of like adopting someone's beloved children; the caring doesn't stop just because the puppy is not in its birth home.

Questions to Ask a Breeder

1. Do you screen your brood bitches for health problems? Which problems?

2. Do you require that the stud owner do the same?

3. How often do you breed a bitch?

4. How many litters do you have per year?

5. Do you check temperament?

6. What problems have you had in your line? (If the answer here is "none" and this person has had several litters, look elsewhere!)

7. Do you give any health or temperament guarantees in writing? What are they and how do they work? (This should be covered in a sales contract which you should read before buying).

8. Do you show your dogs? (Although not a firm requirement, most breeders who care about the breed are trying to improve with each litter. One of the best tests for this is conformation competition.)

These Dane puppies are outstanding in their field! Sunnyside Narcissus, Jonquilla, Peeping Tom, and King Alfred.

A conscientious breeder will be concerned with preserving the quality of the breed and always strives to produce the best puppies possible.

9. What help, if any, will be available for you after the sale, when questions arise?

10. Does the breeder provide complete information on vaccines, wormings and feeding instructions?

11. What about cropped ear after-care?

Go by your instinct. If the place is clean, you can meet at least the dam of the litter, the dogs are clean, happy and healthy and you like the breeder, go for it!

RESCUE DOGS

Just *what is* a "rescue dog"? Most Great Dane clubs maintain a "rescue committee" to help place unwanted Great Danes. Why do these dogs end up in rescue in the first place? Some, like children, are the victims of broken homes and divorce. Others have grown "too big." Still others have not been properly raised and trained, and have become destructive to house and yard. Some have temperament problems or have been badly mistreated or are ill. These last ones are often euthanized, which may be the kindest treatment. In my opinion, the greatest culprit is the breeder himself. Usually we find that the breeder didn't care enough either to match the right dog with the right owner, or to take the dog back when he could no longer be kept by his owners. A good rescue group will evaluate the dog as to health, temperament and suitability to a home with children prior to placement. There is usually only a small donation required, sufficient to cover the maintenance, rehabilitation and spay/neuter cost of the dog. Rescue dogs are not placed without being spayed or neutered. To find out about rescue Danes in your area, contact the Great Dane Club of America at 442 Country View Lane, Garland, Texas 75043.

CHOOSING A PUPPY

You've now decided on the source of your puppy. You've visited the seller a couple of times already and you feel confident and comfortable with your choice. Whether you've decided on a show or pet puppy, it's very important that you have a good relationship with the breeder. There will be many questions needing answers in the future and you should feel free to make calls for help.

At five to seven weeks of age, puppies actively enjoy socializing with their littermates.

During your visits you've probably begun to make your choice of a puppy, or perhaps you already know which pup will go home with you. Although the breeder will certainly assist you in your choice, the final decision is up to you. Whether show or pet, you want a puppy with a friendly, outgoing personality. The one who sits alone in a corner may be appealing, but chances are he will also be shy. Shy dogs can become fear-biters. Depend on the breeder if you lack confidence in your own ability to choose. Breeders who have had years of experience will be able to accurately match the temperament of pups with the temperament of prospective owners. The right puppy for the right home is the goal and is the only way the relationship will happily last.

Choose your Great Dane puppy based on his temperament and how he reacts to you and his littermates. Pick the puppy that best suits your needs and lifestyle.

Conformation is not a consideration in a pet quality Dane. Chances are you will only have a limited selection of puppies that are not considered to be show quality. If you are purchasing a show quality puppy and have no prior experience, listen to the breeder's advice. Besides outstanding conformation, sellers look for that "certain something"—an attitude, a presence, something that makes that particular puppy stand out from his littermates. The seller who knows his own lines well has a fair shot at picking out the pup who will grow into the show contender. However, it isn't uncommon for a well-bred litter to contain several outstanding show prospects, and if this is the case, you could probably make your own choice.

YOUR GROWING Great Dane Puppy

By now you've settled in with your new puppy and a routine is emerging. First thing in the morning he's letting you know it's time to go out and relieve himself. You go out with him, praise him and it's back into the house to fix his breakfast. Assuming you've brought your puppy home shortly after ear cropping, at around ten weeks of age, you've probably already noticed how *fast* he's growing! Where once you could cuddle him in your arms, now you can barely lift him. As mentioned elsewhere, this period of fast growth is also one of the most stressful periods in your puppy's life. Now is the time when a lot can go wrong, while his skeleton is quickly reaching its adult height.

Dane pups start out with an advantage in life if their sire and dam have been properly vaccinated and screened for genetic diseases.

One of the most common problems that can occur (and the one you *pray for* if your dog must have something go wrong), is panosteitis. Most commonly it occurs between four and nine months of age. It's an inflammation of the long bones of the legs. It is also known as "wandering lameness" because it can switch from leg to leg. Panosteitis can cause from very mild almost unnoticeable lameness to intense pain where the dog doesn't even want to get up. Mostly you'll notice slight limping on one and then another leg from week to week. It is a self-limiting problem that most often has disappeared by the time the puppy is around a year old. The cause is unknown.

There are, of course, other growth problems that may occur during this time, but it is not within the scope of this book to go into detail on these. If you have any suspicion that your dog is having a medical problem, your best friend is his veterinarian. I mentioned panosteitis because it's common.

Although a growing Great Dane is very large, this size should not be equated with great strength until he's an adult. A growing Dane puppy is really quite fragile. There

should be no forced exercise of any kind. That doesn't mean that you cannot take your pup for walks on lead or allow him off-lead exercise in a safe area; just don't overdo it. Also be careful if you have other Danes or adult dogs that are as large or larger than the puppy. In rough play your pup may be sent flying as another dog crashes into him. He can be easily hurt under such circumstances, and I'd advise supervised play until he's a lot older.

Some people seem to like to thump, shove and pull a large puppy around in play. Roughly jerking on your puppy's neck while he holds the other end of a tug-of-war toy is definitely *not* a good idea. Neither is roughly pulling on his legs or tail in play. Encourage your Dane pup to chase and fetch a ball. Play tug-of-war *gently*, allowing the pup to do all the pulling while you are more passive.

As your puppy grows, you'll probably notice all kinds of interesting conformational oddities taking place. Most common is when a growth spurt occurs and the rear end is suddenly two inches taller than the front! Cow hocks might appear (turned out toes in the hind legs) or he might develop turned out toes in the front legs. Then they'll get pinched in the rear, appearing to be about four inches wide from behind. Or they'll go through what I call "the flats," appearing to be about four inches wider down the full length of their bodies! Watching a Dane puppy go through the "ganglies" can be frightening, especially if you hope to show him. You'll wonder if he'll *ever* grow into those feet!

Sometimes a puppy will "knuckle over" in his front pastern joints. Most noticeable while sitting, the forelegs

Great Dane puppies go through growth spurts and may look awkward at times. Six-week-old Sunnyside Daffodil has a lot of growing to do!

will appear to bend forward at the pastern (ankle). This is often a phase and should be handled by lowering the protein in his food to around 19 to 20 percent and adding 500 to 1000 mg of vitamin C to his diet morning and night. You should see improvement within a couple of weeks. I'm passing along "anecdotal" information I've recently received from other breeders, as I've not had this problem until my last litter. It scared me and I immediately got on the phone to some of my breeder friends.

If you have more than one Dane puppy, watch them carefully when they play. They can injure themselves or each other if not supervised closely.

Dane puppies often get juvenile acne, just like human teenagers. Purchase a human acne medication and keep his chin dry after eating and drinking. However, this common staph infection will usually disappear as soon as

Great Danes usually make excellent mothers. The care that they lavish on their litter is evident later in happy, even-tempered puppies.

he's past his teens, about one and one-half years or sooner.

Although Danes aren't completely coordinated as puppies, neither should they constantly seem to fall down or lack coordination in their legs. If you feel your puppy is overly clumsy, you should take him to his veterinarian.

As your puppy grows in height, it's a good idea to begin to place his food dish at his shoulder level. By elevating his food dish, you eliminate the volume of air he consumes if he's a fast eater. Water, too, should be offered off the ground.

It is easy to fall in love with an adorable Great Dane puppy, but make sure that the decision to take one home is a carefully considered one.

While your puppy is under a year old, you'll probably notice that his front pasterns (ankles) seem "knobby" and perhaps enlarged around the joint. To the uninformed, this might seem to be abnormal and the puppy is rushed to the vet. This is a normal stage of growth for a Great Dane. The pastern joints remain quite knobby during growth and then smooth out and blend into the rest of the leg with maturity. I've heard of a vet who was so uninformed about this situation in Danes that he diagnosed a disease! He then proceeded to prescribe calcium supplements to correct the problem! The vet actually *caused* a bone problem with this recommendation! Although your vet is often your dog's best friend, it won't hurt for you also to consult a Great Dane breeder. As

It is a good idea to elevate your puppy's food and water dishes. This lessens the amount of air that gets in your Dane's stomach and helps prevent bloat.

breeders, we see these things all the time and know what is and is not normal for a growing Great Dane.

Once your Dane reaches about a year to a year-and-a-half old, he's reached his potential skeletal height. However, he will continue to fill out and mature up until the age of three years.

CARING for Your Great Dane

Several years ago, most breeders recommended feeding high protein food with calcium, phosphorous and vitamin D supplements to giant breed puppies. During this same time, many scientific studies were conducted to try and find out what, if any, influence such practices had on the many growth and bone problems that constantly cropped up in these breeds. It was concluded that feeding a balanced diet and keeping the dog's weight on the low side during growth reduced the incidence of growth and bone problems. Thus it was no longer recommended to add calcium, phosphorous and vitamin D to

Very young puppies have their nutritional needs met through nursing. As they grow, you, the owner, become responsible for providing them with a balanced diet.

the diet—or any other supplement that would cause the delicate balance between these three nutrients to be thrown off. Since I have adopted these feeding practices, I've had virtually no growth or bone problems in my litters.

It isn't enough to simply select a lower protein food for your puppy. You should have some idea of what makes a high *quality* dog food. Protein content must be usable by the dog. If the protein sources are leather dust and chicken feathers, the dog isn't going to utilize them. Basically, if a food is a chicken-based food, it will list whole chicken or chicken meal as its first ingredient. The first ingredient listed on a dog food bag makes up the highest percentage of that food. The next highest percentage of ingredients is listed next, and so on down the line. Poultry *by-products* usually consist of beaks, feathers and bones – not much nutrition there.

Feed your Great Dane puppies a quality food so they get the nutrients they need.

It's also helpful to know that minerals listed on the bag should be chelated in order to be fully usable by the dog's system. Just because you see certain ingredients on the list does not ensure that the dog will be able to use them in the offered form. Some vitamins lose their potency when subjected to the high temperatures used in processing. A top quality food will use other means to add these delicate vitamins later, after the food has been cooked and cooled. The vitamins such as vitamin C are sprayed onto the cooled product, thus retaining their potency.

A few dog food companies take the time to listen to input from breeders and trainers and incorporate this input into the formulation of their dog foods. For instance, some manufacturers now add probiotics to their dog food. Probiotics are enzymes that help the dog to better digest its food. In the case of Great Danes, who are so vulnerable to bloat, this can only be a plus. I've fed this type of dog food to my gang for several years and they no longer clear out the room every five minutes with their noxious gaseous odors! I also add

A steady supply of fresh, clean water is essential to your Great Dane's well-being.

powdered probiotics to the food. Less gas in their tummies has to be good!

I have mentioned all of the above to help you realize that it is false economy in the long run to buy the cheapest dog food available. There are several quality dog foods available for your Great Dane. I must also tell you that I am not a nutrition expert, nor am I a veterinarian, but I've seen the results of feeding these foods in the outcome of my last several litters and I am a believer! I also tend to prefer foods that have a more "natural" base. Foods that use chemical preservatives such as ethoxyothin should be avoided!

Hopefully the breeder has been feeding your little one on good food. If not, and you wish to change him over, do it gradually over a period of five to seven days. You should be informed as to how much your puppy has been eating. You should also be provided with enough of the food to make a gradual change to whatever food you will be feeding, if applicable. The amount of food your puppy eats isn't as important as how he looks. You should gauge the amount to feed by his physical appearance. You want to be able to just feel his ribs. He should be kept no fatter than this. Depending on his age, he should be eating from two to three meals a day. Most of my pups are on two meals a day by the time they're around eight weeks. I usually gauge it by how enthusiastically they eat their noon meal. Once they start leaving quite a bit of it, I switch them to two meals a day. Danes should be kept on a minimum of two meals daily for life.

If something happens to your puppy's mother, you may have to take on the responsibility of feeding him while he is young.

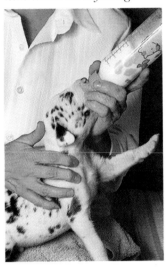

To give a vague idea of amounts to feed, I'm currently feeding a six-week-old about a cup and a quarter of dry kibble mixed with about a 1/4-cup of canned food three times a day. At this early age you must be very alert to the body condition as it isn't uncommon to have to increase the amounts of food almost daily to keep up with growth! Many Dane puppies at eight weeks are eating about three cups of food morning and evening. My six-month-old bitch is currently eating four cups morning and night. Her eight-year-old grandmother exists very nicely on half that amount! The average for my in-betweeners is about three cups morning and night. A lot depends on age, activity level and size. Most dog foods give a guideline. You can adjust the amounts up or down in quantity as needed.

Because I tend to spoil my dogs and like to give my Danes treats, I add a small amount of canned food to each meal. I also will add table scraps when available and occasionally some yogurt (mainly when someone is on antibiotics), cottage cheese or eggs. Since all these additives are capable of unbalancing a balanced meal, a good rule of thumb is to add no more than 15 percent of the total dry being fed. This will not cause the food to be unbalanced. All this is mixed with a bit of water. Most of my dogs have always been walking garbage cans when it comes to food, but occasionally there will be a picky one. If you have a puppy that isn't a good eater, don't make the mistake of doctoring the food or leaving it available for a long time. If they don't clean it up within 20 minutes, take it away.

Some people recommend that Danes not be allowed water at all times, but I've never taken water away from mine. I think they will tend to over-drink if they *don't* have water when they want it.

Some Dane owners supplement their dogs' diets with vitamin C. Although dogs will manufacture their own vitamin C in most cases, it probably can't hurt to give them a reasonable boost of C. Vitamin C is water soluble and will not become toxic if fed a reasonable amount — about 500 to 1000 mg per day is the usual dosage.

All my dogs are fed a diet of about 23% protein throughout their lives. The only exception is that I will switch my brood bitch to a higher protein food while she's gestating the litter and lactating. The pups will even share this with her in the very early weaning stage up until the really fast growth begins at around four or five weeks. They go directly to 22 percent protein and even lower if I see any knuckling over in the pasterns or other potential problems.

It is a good idea to elevate your Dane's food dish to about the height of the point of his shoulder. This helps prevent the gulping of air while eating, a suspected contributor to bloat. You can place his dish on a folding chair, purchase a feeding station made for this purpose, or make a wire holder that weaves through the mesh of a chain-link fence, which is what I've done.

GROOMING

One of the best aspects about owning a Great Dane is that they need very little in the way of grooming. Having short, thick hair means that there's no tangling or matting. A weekly going-over with a soft, rubber curry comb and a soft brush, combined with the occasional bath when dirty, is all that's needed. Toenails, of course, are kept short and ears and teeth are cleaned as needed.

Get your puppy used to the grooming procedures when he is small by giving him a bath in warm water and brushing him often. Cold water will not make your puppy eager for his next bath. In the past, in nice weather, I've hooked a hose up to an indoor faucet with both hot and cold water and then bathed the dogs outdoors with the hose. Now I have a wonderful place in my home with a walk-in dog shower, complete with Scooby Doo wallpaper!

Toenails should be clipped weekly. Use either a nail clipper made especially for dogs or a grinder. Be careful not to cut the quick, which is the vein in your Dane's toenails. It hurts the dog and causes the toenail to bleed. The grinder is great because it will cauterize the blood vessel should you cut the quick. Styptic powder will also help to curb the bleeding.

Your Great Dane's ears can be gently cleaned with cotton balls or

When trimming your dog's toenails, be careful not to cut the quick (the blood vein inside the nail) or they will bleed.

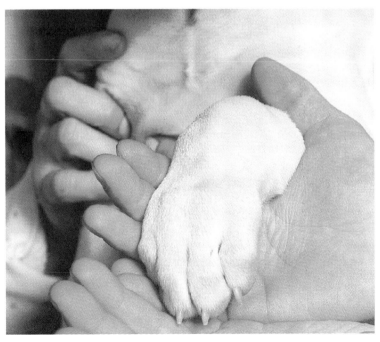

cotton swabs dampened in ear-cleaning solution or hydrogen peroxide.

CROPPED EARS AND THEIR CARE

To crop or not to crop is often an emotional issue. If you have the choice, it should be an informed one. Most dogs in the show ring are cropped: however, this is *not* a requirement for showing. The Great Dane standard of perfection gives a description for both cropped and uncropped ears.

Uncropped Ears

First of all, it's interesting to realize that in the wild, there are no animals with drop ears! The erect ear is nature's way of keeping an open ear canal so that air can reach inside. This helps prevent infection. Drop ears are more susceptible to infection than erect ears. They are also more likely to develop a hematoma if the head is shaken hard. This happens when the ear tips "snap" like a snapped towel and cause the blood vessels in the tips of the ears to break. They bleed into the ear tissue and cause a painful swelling. Sometimes this swelling breaks open when the dog shakes its head and blood flies everywhere! Hematomas are difficult to heal and often keep re-opening.

Although cropping is not necessary for a show dog, uncropped Danes have a different "look" compared to cropped Danes. The alert attitude of an uncropped dog pales in comparison to the same attitude on a cropped dog. All else being equal on these dogs, a judge might tend to lean toward the cropped animal when making his or her placements.

The decision to crop your Great Dane puppy's ears is a personal one. Be sure you are well informed about the procedure before making your choice.

Cropped Ears

When people object to cropping ears, it's often because they've seen a poor job done by someone who has no idea of the proper way to crop an ear. Have your Dane's ears cropped by a veterinarian who has experience with the breed. Cropping is often learned by veterinarians who were themselves breeders of a cropped breed, or who were properly taught by another veterinarian who has been doing show crops for years. He may even have been taught by a breeder! Great pain and disfigurement can be caused if the ear is not properly cut, stitched and either racked or

Have your Dane's ears cropped only by a knowledgeable and experienced veterinarian.

The standard for the Great Dane does not require cropped ears. This Dane sports the soft, natural look.

taped to some kind of support. And if the after-care giver has no knowledge of how to properly tape and train cropped ears, a great deal of unnecessary damage and pain can be caused. Chances are that the breeder has cropped the litter and has used a talented veterinarian. If done by a veterinarian, there is little pain involved; certainly no more than the pain of a hematoma.

Although today's ear cropping is done primarily for looks, its original intent was a practical one— to prevent the ears from being torn during the hunt.

There is more to having a Dane with beautiful, cropped, properly standing ears than simply purchasing a cropped puppy or having him cropped after purchase. The actual crop is only half the battle. The rest is the after-care, which usually lasts until five or six months of age but can continue up to a year or even longer! If you live close enough to the seller, he or

52

she will often continue to tape and train the ears for you, or will teach you how to do it properly. If you don't live close enough to the seller and no one close to you can be recommended, you're on your own. I've included instructions here that I hope will assist you in this task.

Ear taping consists of taping the ears in such a way that they stand erect. The tape is usually left on for a week to ten days, removed for a couple of days and then reapplied. This is done consistently until the ears are standing. It's time-consuming but in my opinion, worth it.

Different vets use different methods of stabilizing the ears immediately after cropping. Few will change their methods because you ask, but here are some of the ways it's done. My personal experience has always been with "racks." They are formed out of stiff wire (often wire coat hangers) and shaped so the ears can be taped erect to them directly on top of the head. If properly taped, they cause little discomfort to the puppy. They are left on for two weeks. My only real objection to racks is that they can become caught on things. I've seen pups get them stuck in the ground and severely twist their necks while playing. I had one of my own do this and she turned out to be a wobbler. It may have just been coincidence, but I've always felt that this experience had something to do with her developing this disease.

If you properly care for your Great Dane's ears after cropping, the alert, dignified appearance that some owners desire will be achieved.

Some vets will tape the ears flat over the top of the head and then apply a bandage. I don't care for this method, as I think it tends to cause the ears to "cup" over the top of the head when they're taken down. I've only seen this done, I've never had a pup treated with this method.

The other method I've seen uses Styrofoam cups stacked one atop the other and then reinforced with tape. They are set on top of the head and the ears are taped directly to their sides. I think that this looks like the best method of all. People I've discussed it with recommend it highly. The cups are loose enough to "give" when pushed around in play, and being very lightweight, the pups seem to hardly know they're there.

After-Care of the Ear

Once your puppy has been cropped and the racks are off, it's time for the after-care to begin. Without proper after-care, the ears are unlikely to stand properly. Be sure that the ears are completely healed. If there are one or two scabby areas, be sure not to tape over them.

There are probably as many after-care methods as there are breeders. The two basic differences in most methods are that one completely encloses the ear and the ear canal and the other leaves it open to the air. I don't care for the enclosed method as not only is it extremely irritating to the puppy, but it also causes infection or a major case of the "gooeys." The gooeys are when you get a disgusting gray goo forming under the more enclosed areas of tape. I much prefer and recommend any method that leaves the ear open to the air. I've included my method and directions below.

You will need:

1. A length of 1/2-inch fabric stay material (found in a fabric store). Cut these long enough to reach from the top of the "bump" of the ear to just past the ear tip. See Figure 1.

2. Medical-type adhesive tape. A 1-inch and a 1 1/2-inch roll. You can find this at a hospital supply store and some drug stores carry it also.

3. Tincture of Benzoin, found at a pharmacy.

4. Cotton swabs.

5. Bandage scissors.

6. Medicated powder to promote healing and relieve itchiness.

7. Rubbing alcohol.

8. Cotton balls.

9. Two one-inch plastic hair curlers, cut about 1 1/4-inch long.

Before you get started, have all your supplies on hand and ask someone to help you. That person can hold the puppy and hand you supplies as needed. Follow this procedure: After you've cut the curlers, use your scissors to smooth any rough edges from the cut ends. Take the wide tape and cover the rollers completely, tucking the excess at the ends inside the rollers. Set aside.

Cut two pieces from the one-inch tape that protrude about 1/4-inch past the stay material you've already cut. You will notice that the stay has a slight curve. You want the inside of the curve to press against the inside of the ear. Lay one piece of tape down sticky-side up. Center the stay on the tape with the convex side against the tape. Take the next piece of tape and lay it on top of the stay, sticky-side up, making a "sandwich" of tape, then stay, then tape. Repeat with the second piece of tape and set aside. Next, cut two pieces of one-inch tape long enough to roll once around the roller and extend approximately nine inches beyond. Do this to both rollers and set aside.

Caring for your Dane's ears after cropping is a very involved and time consuming process. Heather is thanking her owner for taking such good care of her!

Preparing the ears. Clean the ears well with alcohol and dry thoroughly. Next, using a couple of cotton swabs, paint the ear with the tincture of Benzoin. Cover the inside of the ear from the "bump" (see Figure 1) to the tip. Clean the outside of the ear to the tip and pay particular attention to the outside of the base. Allow to dry until tacky, about two to three minutes.

Next, take one of the stays and set it into the inside of the ear just resting on the "bump." Smooth and apply pressure until stuck firmly (Figure 2).

Shake a small amount of the medicated powder in the little fold at the base of the ear on top of the head. This will help prevent the "gooeys" that usually start here.

Take the curler with the long tape attached and set the base just above the "bump" with the long tape pointing in towards the center of the head. It is important to keep tension on the ear at this point. You want the base pulled out from the head

ILLUSTRATION

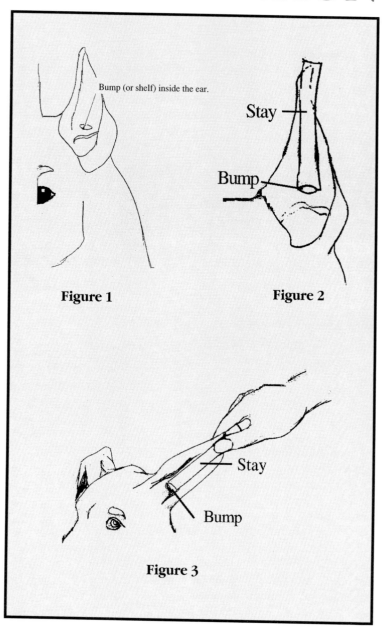

Bump (or shelf) inside the ear.

Figure 1

Stay

Bump

Figure 2

Stay

Bump

Figure 3

OF AFTER CARE

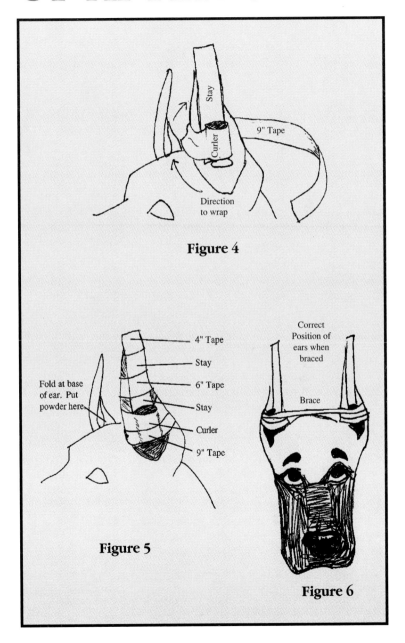

Figure 4

- 4" Tape
- Stay
- 6" Tape
- Stay
- Curler
- 9" Tape

Fold at base of ear. Put powder here.

Figure 5

Correct Position of ears when braced

Brace

Figure 6

so you can tape it properly in order for it to stand (Figure 3). Wrap in the direction of the small ear fold at the base of the ear. Wrap snug but not too tight (Figure 4).

From the one-inch tape cut a nine-inch, a six-inch and a four-inch (approximately) long piece. Wrap the nine-inch piece overlapping the base of the curler, just below the first wrap, making sure to keep the tension on the ear during this procedure. The six-inch piece goes around the ear in the middle of the ear and the four-inch piece wraps the very tip (Figure 5).

Although their size may suggest otherwise, the Great Dane is a sensitive dog that needs gentle handling and care.

Repeat the procedure on the other ear. (Note that the ear will be pulled into the curler more than shown in the illustration.) For the first couple of tapings after cropping (that is, after the incisions have healed, sutures are removed and the rack is off), it's a good idea to brace the ears across the top of the head.

Bracing the taped ears. Cut a piece of "stay" material wide enough to span between the ears without rubbing the ears themselves, usually about three to four inches. Cut a piece of one-inch tape long enough to reach from one ear to the other, circle the ear, return to the first ear, circle it, and wrap about half way back to the other ear. Ears should be held erect, and allowed to turn into a naturally held position, usually slightly out from the side of the head. Ask your helper to hold the ears while you tape. Start taping at the front of one ear, span to the other, circle it around the back of this ear, to the front span, then insert the stay and sandwich it between the two pieces of tape. Continue the tape around the second ear and back across the front. Be very careful not to twist or turn the ears out of their natural resting position. Cut a short (about two-inch) piece of one-inch tape and wrap around the span between the ears a couple times so the stay will remain in place. You're done! Leave ears taped about a week, then take tape off and allow ears to rest for a day. Repeat until the ears are standing.

CRATE AND BASIC TRAINING

Great Danes are *not* backyard dogs. They are sensitive individuals who need to live in the home with their families. A

Your Great Dane will use his crate as his own sanctuary from the rest of the world, and it helps to make housebreaking your pet a much easier job.

caring breeder will never sell to someone who won't keep his Dane in this manner. However, at the same time, while they are still puppies– big puppies at that, and full of mischief– some kind of restraint is necessary. This is where a crate comes to the rescue. Crates are not cruel! Crates become like the dog's own private room where he can go to get away from a bustling household for a quiet nap. Crates make housebreaking a snap because no self-respecting Great Dane wants to soil his bed. Crates also protect your home and belongings when the dog must be left unattended for a few hours at a time.

When you purchase a crate, keep in mind the eventual size of the dog. There are two basic types; wire and enclosed metal, or fiberglass construction. Personally I prefer the wire as it allows the air to circulate freely. I keep a crate in the bedroom when I'm housebreaking a puppy. That way he's still part of the family, but I know there will be no overnight messes.

A Dane is a big and active puppy. He must not be confined in a crate for hours at a time. Overnight is fine, but during the day, he needs to exercise. If you can allow him the run of your back yard with access to shelter during the day when you cannot be home, this is ideal. A six-foot chain link fence that he can't dig underneath is perfect. If you live in a cold climate, it is necessary to provide some source of heat if the dog must remain outdoors for long periods of time. If you have other older dogs, it's a good idea to keep them separate from the puppy when you're not home to supervise. This is especially true if they're bigger than the pup. Although you probably think of a Dane as a dog that can "take it," they are really quite fragile when young. It doesn't take a lot to cause serious injury to young growing bones and unclosed physis (the growth plate at the end of the bones.)

Like every member of your family, your Great Dane puppy must know the rules of the house and obey them.

Since your puppy will be considered a family member, like the rest of the family he must have rules to follow. Training should begin when you first bring him home. If you have a certain place in the yard you want him to use to relieve himself, take him there immediately, stay with him until he does his business and then praise the daylights out of him. Take him into the house and allow him to explore while you supervise. It isn't too soon to begin teaching him what the word "no" means. If he's to stay off the furniture, let him know it from the start. Consistency is the key to successful training. Get him used to his crate right away. If he has plenty of chew toys and "stuffies" (soft cloth toys or those wonderful things made out of phony sheepskin), and knows you're nearby, he'll likely drift off almost immediately. But please, *No Rawhide*! It can cause intestinal blockage. Roar-Hide™ by Nylabone® is a safe alternative to rawhide. It is melted and molded into the shape of a bone and will not break or chip in your dog's mouth.

Danes are easily housetrained. Just take your puppy out to potty when he lets you know it's time, stay with him and praise him when he goes, and then take him back to his bed. Young puppies usually need to relieve themselves right after eating, as soon as they awaken, and after strenuous play. If you are faithful to these rules, you won't *believe* how quickly he becomes housetrained!

Because Great Danes are a giant breed, it follows that they make giant poops! This might be a consideration for someone who has only had little dogs. A Dane's poop might weigh as much as a little dog! Well, perhaps not really, but there definitely is more of it to clean up.

One rule of thumb when crate training: never, never, *NEVER* use the crate as punishment! The crate must remain the one place that is non-threateningly his, always.

To combat boredom and relieve your Dane's natural desire to chew, there's nothing better than a Roar-Hide™. Unlike common rawhide, this bone won't turn into a gooey mess when chewed on, so your dog won't choke on small pieces of it, and your carpet won't be stained by it. The Roar-Hide™ is completely edible and is high in protein (over 86%) and low in fat (less than 1/3 of 1%). The super-sized Roar-Hide™ is just right for your Great Dane. Available at your local pet shop.

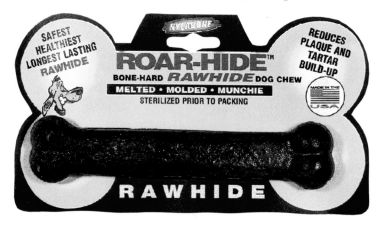

Introduce your Dane puppy to different people and animals. This will help him become well-socialized and adaptable to all kinds of situations.

I am not an obedience trainer and I will not go into this subject at any great length. However, I will tell you that it is advisable to take a training class with your Dane. Any puppy needs to learn rules. A Great Dane puppy who is allowed to be the "boss" will cause a lot of problems in your household once he is an adult and ten times the size. This is the dog who will inevitably experience behavior problems and will end up in multiple homes or sent to the animal shelter.

Be sure to properly socialize your puppy by exposing him to life outside your home. Take him to shopping malls and encourage strangers to approach and pet him. Once he has had all his vaccines, take him to parks and to puppy matches. Enter him in a puppy kindergarten class. Teach him basic manners towards other dogs and people at home, such as not to jump up on people and not to nip or bite when playing. As long as the puppy grows up knowing that *you* are the boss, you should encounter few problems.

Sport of Purebred Dogs

Welcome to the exciting and sometimes frustrating sport of dogs. No doubt you are trying to learn more about dogs or you wouldn't be deep into this book. This section covers the basics that may entice you, further your knowledge and help you to understand the dog world. If you decide to give showing, obedience or any other dog activities a try, then I suggest you seek further help from the appropriate source.

Dog showing has been a very popular sport for a long time and has been taken quite seriously by some. Others only enjoy it as a hobby.

The Kennel Club in England was formed in 1859, the American Kennel Club was established in 1884 and the Canadian Kennel Club was formed in 1888. The purpose of these clubs was to register purebred dogs and maintain their Stud Books. In the beginning, the concept of registering dogs was not readily accepted. More than 36 million dogs have been enrolled in the AKC Stud Book since its inception in 1888. Presently the kennel clubs not only register dogs but adopt and enforce rules and regulations governing dog shows, obedience trials and field trials. Over the years they have fostered and encouraged interest in the health and welfare of the purebred dog. They routinely donate funds to veterinary research for study on genetic disorders.

Practicing to show your puppy can be a great way to start him with basic training and build his confidence.

Below are the addresses of the kennel clubs in the United States, Great Britain and Canada.

The American Kennel Club
51 Madison Avenue
New York, NY 10010
(Their registry is located at: 5580 Centerview Drive, STE 200, Raleigh, NC 27606-3390)

Seven-week-old Perry gets a lesson in "stand"—it's as easy as nibbling on a treat.

The Kennel Club
1 Clarges Street
Piccadilly, London, WIY 8AB, England

The Canadian Kennel Club
111 Eglinton Avenue
East Toronto, Ontario M6S 4V7
Canada

Today there are numerous activities that are enjoyable for both the dog and the handler. Some of the activities include conformation showing, obedience competition, tracking, agility, the Canine Good Citizen Certificate, and a wide range of instinct tests that vary from breed to breed. Where you start depends upon your goals, which early on may not be readily apparent.

Puppy Kindergarten

Every puppy will benefit from this class. PKT is the foundation for all future dog activities from conformation to "couch potatoes." Pet owners should make an effort to attend even if they never expect to show their dog. The class is designed for puppies about three months of age with graduation at approximately five months of age. All the puppies will be in the same age group and, even though some may be a little unruly, there should not be any real problem. This class will teach the puppy some beginning obedience. As in all obedience classes, the owner learns how to train his own dog. The PKT class gives the puppy the opportunity to interact with other puppies in the same age group and exposes him to strangers, which is very important. Some dogs grow up with behavior problems, one of them being fear of strangers. As you can see, there can be much to gain from this class.

There are some basic obedience exercises that every dog should learn. Some of these can be started with puppy kindergarten.

Sit

One way of teaching the sit is to have your dog on your left side with the leash in your right hand, close to the collar. Pull up on the leash and at the same time reach around his hindlegs with your left hand and tuck them in. As you are doing this say, "Beau, sit." Always use the dog's name when you give an active command. Some owners like to use a treat, holding it over the dog's head. The dog will need to sit to get the treat. Encourage the dog to hold the sit for a few seconds, which will eventually be the beginning of the Sit/Stay. Depending on how cooperative he is, you can rub him under the chin or stroke his back. It is a good time to establish eye contact.

Down

Sit the dog on your left side and kneel down beside him with the leash in your right hand. Reach over him with your left hand and grasp his left foreleg. With your right hand, take his right foreleg and pull his legs forward while you say, "Beau, down." If he tries to get up, lean on his shoulder to encourage

Teaching your Great Dane to sit is one of the basic commands in obedience training.

Ch. Haltmeier's Zoe, owned by Betty Wilson, shown here winning Best of Winners, which means she topped all the dogs and bitches in the regular classes.

him to stay down. It will relax your dog if you stroke his back while he is down. Try to encourage him to stay down for a few seconds as preparation for the Down/Stay.

Heel

The definition of heeling is the dog walking under control at your left heel. Your puppy will learn controlled walking in the puppy kindergarten class, which will eventually lead to heeling. The command is "Beau, heel," and you start off briskly with your left foot. Your leash is in your right hand and your left hand is holding it about halfway down. Your left hand should be able to control the leash and there should be a little slack in it. You want him to walk with you with your leg somewhere between his nose and his shoulder. You need to encourage him to stay with you, not forging (in front of you) or lagging behind you. It is best to keep him on a fairly short lead. Do not allow the lead to become tight. It is far better to give him a little jerk when necessary and remind him to heel. When you come to a halt, be prepared physically to make him sit. It takes practice to become coordinated. There are excellent books on training that you may wish to purchase. Your instructor should be able to recommend one for you.

Recall

A well-trained Great Dane is not only a pleasure to his owners, but to strangers as well.

This quite possibly is the most important exercise you will ever teach. It should be a pleasant experience. The puppy may learn to do random recalls while being attached to a long line such as a clothes line. Later the exercise will start with the dog sitting and staying until called. The command is "Beau, come." Let your command be happy. You want your dog to come willingly and faithfully. The recall could save his life if he sneaks out the door. In practicing the recall, let him jump on you or touch you before you reach for him. If he is shy, then kneel down to his level. Reaching for the insecure dog could frighten him, and he may not be willing to come again in the future. Lots of praise and a treat would be in order whenever you do a recall. Under no circumstances should you ever correct your dog when he has come to you. Later in formal obedience your dog will be required to sit in front of you after recalling and then go to heel position.

CONFORMATION

Conformation showing is our oldest dog show sport. This type of showing is based on the dog's appearance—that is his

structure, movement and attitude. When considering this type of showing, you need to be aware of your breed's standard

With your dog on a lead, practice recall exercises. Always praise your Dane when he comes to you, so he will look forward to being at your side.

and be able to evaluate your dog compared to that standard. The breeder of your puppy or other experienced breeders would be good sources for such an evaluation. Puppies can go through lots of changes over a period of time. I always say most puppies start out as promising hopefuls and then after maturing may be disappointing as show candidates. Even so this should not deter them from being excellent pets.

Usually conformation training classes are offered by the local kennel or obedience clubs. These are excellent places for training puppies. The puppy should be able to walk on a lead before entering such a class. Proper ring procedure and technique for posing (stacking) the dog will be demonstrated as well as gaiting the dog. Usually certain patterns are used in the ring such as the triangle or the "L." Conformation class, like the PKT class, will give your youngster the opportunity to socialize with different breeds of dogs and humans too.

In conformation shows, the dogs are evaluated on how close they come to the standard, or ideal, for the breed.

It takes some time to learn the routine of conformation showing. Usually one starts at the puppy matches which may be AKC Sanctioned or Fun Matches. These matches are generally for puppies from two or three months to a year old, and there may be classes for the adult over the age of 12 months. Similar to point shows, the classes are divided by sex and after completion of the classes in that breed or variety, the class winners compete for Best of Breed or Variety. The winner goes on to compete in the Group and the Group winners compete for Best in Match. No championship points are awarded for match wins.

A few matches can be great training for puppies even though there is no intention to go on showing. Matches enable the puppy to meet new people and be handled by a stranger—the judge. It is also a change of environment, which broadens the horizon for both dog and handler. Matches and other dog activities boost the confidence of the handler and especially the younger handlers.

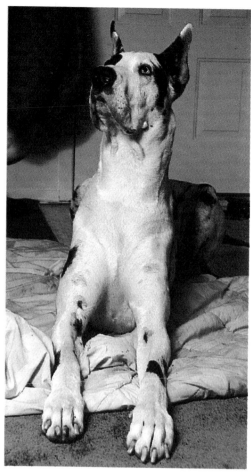

Your dog should always know who is the boss, especially a breed as large as the Great Dane. This Dane awaits his next command from his master.

Earning an AKC championship is built on a point system, which is different from Great Britain. To become an AKC Champion of Record the dog must earn 15 points. The number of points earned each time depends upon the number of dogs in competition. The number of points available at each show depends upon the breed, its sex and the location of the show. The United States is divided into ten AKC zones. Each zone has its own set of points. The purpose of the zones is to try to equalize the points available from breed to breed and area to area. The AKC adjusts the point scale annually.

The number of points that can be won at a show are between one and five. Three-, four- and five-point wins are considered majors. Not only does the dog need 15 points won under three different judges, but those points must include two majors under two different judges. Canada also works on a point system but majors are not required.

Dogs always show before bitches. The classes available to those seeking points are: Puppy (which may be divided into 6 to 9 months and 9 to 12 months); 12 to 18 months; Novice; Bred-by-Exhibitor; American-bred; and Open. The class winners of the same sex of each breed or variety compete against each other for Winners Dog and Winners Bitch. A Reserve Winners Dog and Reserve Winners Bitch are also awarded but do not carry any points unless the Winners win is disallowed by AKC. The Winners Dog and Bitch compete with the specials (those dogs that have attained championship) for Best of Breed or Variety, Best of Winners and Best of Opposite Sex. It is possible to pick up an extra point or even a major if the points are higher for the defeated winner than those of Best of Winners. The latter would get the higher total from the defeated winner.

At an all-breed show, each Best of Breed or Variety winner will go on to his respective Group and then the Group winners will compete against each other for Best in Show. There are seven Groups: Sporting, Hounds, Working, Terriers, Toys, Non-Sporting and Herding. Obviously there are no Groups at specialty shows (those shows that have only one breed or a show such as the American Spaniel Club's Flushing Spaniel Show, which is for all flushing spaniel breeds).

Earning a championship in England is somewhat different since they do not have a point system. Challenge Certificates are awarded if the judge feels the dog is deserving regardless of the number of dogs in competition. A dog must earn three Challenge Certificates under three different judges, with at least one of these Certificates being won after the age of 12 months. Competition is very strong and entries may be higher than they are in the U.S. The Kennel Club's Challenge Certificates are only available at Championship Shows.

In England, The Kennel Club regulations require that certain dogs, Border Collies and Gundog breeds, qualify in a working capacity (i.e., obedience or field trials) before becoming a full Champion. If they do not qualify in the working aspect, then they are designated a Show Champion, which is equivalent to the AKC's Champion of Record. A Gundog may be granted the title of Field Trial Champion (FT Ch.) if it passes all the tests in the field but would also have to qualify in conformation before becoming a full Champion. A Border Collie that earns the title of Obedience Champion (Ob Ch.) must also qualify in the conformation ring before becoming a Champion.

The U.S. doesn't have a designation full Champion but does award for Dual and Triple Champions. The Dual Champion must be a Champion of Record, and either Champion Tracker, Herding Champion, Obedience Trial Champion or Field Champion. Any dog that has been awarded the titles of Champion of Record, and any two of the following: Champion Tracker, Herding Champion, Obedience Trial Champion or Field Champion, may be designated as a Triple Champion.

Great Danes, like this fawn Ch. Sunnyside Cricket, are shown as part of the Working Group at AKC dog shows.

The shows in England seem to put more emphasis on breeder judges than those in the U.S. There is much competition within the breeds. Therefore the quality of the individual breeds should be very good. In the United States we tend to have more "all around judges" (those that judge multiple breeds) and use the breeder judges at the specialty shows. Breeder judges are more familiar with their own breed since they are actively breeding that breed or did so at one time. Americans emphasize Group and Best in Show wins and promote them accordingly.

It is my understanding that the shows in England can be very large and extend over several days, with the Groups being scheduled on different days. I believe there is only one all-breed show in the U.S. that extends over two days, the Westminster Kennel Club Show. In our country we have cluster shows, where several different clubs will use the same show site over consecutive days.

Westminster Kennel Club is our most prestigious show although the entry is limited to 2500. In recent years, entry has been limited to Champions. This show is more formal than the majority of the shows with the judges wearing formal attire and the handlers fashionably dressed. In most instances the quality of the dogs is superb. After all, it is a show of Champions. It is a good show to study the AKC registered breeds and is by far the most exciting—especially since it is televised! WKC is one of the few shows in this country that is still benched. This means the dog must be in his benched area during the show hours except when he is being groomed, in the ring, or being exercised.

Typically, the handlers are very particular about their appearances. They are careful not to wear something that will detract from their dog but will perhaps enhance it. American ring procedure is quite formal compared to that of other countries. I remember being reprimanded by a judge because I made a suggestion to a friend holding my second dog outside the ring. I certainly could have used more discretion so I would not call attention to myself. There is a certain etiquette expected

Handlers must wear practical and comfortable clothing that does not detract from the dog's appearance.

This is future Ch. Sunnyside Desperado at four-and-one-half months with his owner Vicki Gardner, practicing behind the scenes.

between the judge and exhibitor and among the other exhibitors. Of course it is not always the case but the judge is supposed to be polite, not engaging in small talk or even acknowledging that he knows the handler. I understand that there is a more informal and relaxed atmosphere at the shows in other countries. For instance, the dress code is more casual. I can see where this might be more fun for the exhibitor and especially for the novice. This country is very handler-oriented in many of the breeds. It is true, in most instances, that the experienced professional handler can present the dog better and will have a feel for what a judge likes.

In England, Crufts is The Kennel Club's own show and is most assuredly the largest dog show in the world. They've been known to have an entry of nearly 20,000, and the show lasts four days. Entry is only gained by qualifying through winning in specified classes at another Championship Show. Westminster is strictly conformation, but Crufts exhibitors and spectators enjoy not only conformation but obedience, agility and a multitude of exhibitions as well. Obedience was admitted in 1957 and agility in 1983.

If you are handling your own dog, please give some consideration to your apparel. For sure the dress code at matches is more informal than the point shows. However, you should wear something a little more appropriate than beach attire or ragged jeans and bare feet. If you check out the handlers and see what is presently fashionable, you'll catch on. Men usually dress with a shirt and tie and a nice sports coat. Whether you are male or female, you will want to wear comfortable clothes and shoes. You need to be able to run with your dog and you certainly don't want to take a chance of falling and hurting yourself. Heaven forbid, if nothing else, you'll upset your dog. Women usually wear a dress or two-piece outfit, preferably with pockets to carry bait, comb, brush, etc. In this case men are the lucky ones with all their pockets. Ladies, think about where your dress will be if you need to kneel on the floor and also think about running. Does it allow freedom to do so?

Years ago, after toting around all the baby paraphernalia, I found toting the dog and necessities a breeze. You need to take along dog; crate; ex pen (if you use one); extra newspaper; water pail and water; all required grooming equipment, including hair dryer and extension cord; table; chair for you; bait for dog and lunch for you and friends; and, last but not least, clean up materials, such as plastic bags, paper towels, and perhaps a bath towel and some shampoo—just in case. Don't forget your entry confirmation and directions to the show.

If you are showing in obedience, then you will want to wear pants. Many of our top obedience handlers wear pants that are color-coordinated with their dogs. The philosophy is that imperfections in the black dog will be less obvious next to your black pants.

Whether you are showing in conformation, Junior Showmanship or obedience, you need to watch the clock and be sure you are not late. It is customary to pick up your conformation armband a few minutes before the start of the class. They will not wait for you and if you are on the show grounds and not in the ring, you will upset everyone. It's a little more complicated picking up your obedience armband if you show later in the class. If you have not picked up your armband and they get to your number, you may not be allowed to show. It's best to pick up your armband early, but then you may show earlier than expected if other handlers don't pick up. Customarily all conflicts should be discussed with the judge prior to the start of the class.

Junior Showmanship

The Junior Showmanship Class is a wonderful way to build self confidence even if there are no aspirations of staying with the dog-show game later in life. Frequently, Junior Showmanship becomes the background of those who become successful exhibitors/handlers in the future. In some instances it is taken very seriously, and success is measured in terms of wins. The Junior Handler is judged solely on his ability and skill in presenting his dog. The dog's conformation is not to be considered by the judge. Even so the condition and grooming of the dog may be a reflection upon the handler.

A family affair! Sunnyside Colorado Columbine, with Ed, Heather and Matthew Dillon, winning Best of Winners at the Great Dane Club of Greater Denver specialty show.

Usually the matches and point shows include different classes. The Junior Handler's dog may be entered in a breed or obedience class and even shown by another person in that class. Junior Showmanship classes are usually divided by age and perhaps sex. The age is determined by the handler's age on the day of the show. The classes are:

The Canine Good Citizen Test, a program sponsored by the AKC, encourages owners to train their dogs to be friendly and well-mannered, especially towards people and other animals.

Novice Junior for those at least ten and under 14 years of age who at time of entry closing have not won three first places in a Novice Class at a licensed or member show.

Novice Senior for those at least 14 and under 18 years of age who at the time of entry closing have not won three first places in a Novice Class at a licensed or member show.

Open Junior for those at least ten and under 14 years of age who at the time of entry closing have won at least three first places in a Novice Junior Showmanship Class at a licensed or member show with competition present.

Open Senior for those at least 14 and under 18 years of age who at time of entry closing have won at least three first places in a Novice Junior Showmanship Class at a licensed or member show with competition present.

Junior Handlers must include their AKC Junior Handler number on each show entry. This needs to be obtained from the AKC.

CANINE GOOD CITIZEN

The AKC sponsors a program to encourage dog owners to train their dogs. Local clubs perform the pass/fail tests, and dogs who pass are awarded a Canine Good Citizen Certificate. Proof of vaccination is required at the time of participation. The test includes:

1. Accepting a friendly stranger.
2. Sitting politely for petting.
3. Appearance and grooming.
4. Walking on a loose leash.
5. Walking through a crowd.
6. Sit and down on command/staying in place.
7. Come when called.
8. Reaction to another dog.

9. Reactions to distractions.

10. Supervised separation.

If more effort was made by pet owners to accomplish these exercises, fewer dogs would be cast off to the humane shelter.

OBEDIENCE

Obedience is necessary, without a doubt, but it can also become a wonderful hobby or even an obsession. In my opinion, obedience classes and competition can provide wonderful companionship, not only with your dog but with your classmates or fellow competitors. It is always gratifying to discuss your dog's problems with others who have had similar experiences. The AKC acknowledged Obedience around 1936, and it has changed tremendously even though many of the exercises are basically the same. Today, obedience competition is just that—very competitive. Even so, it is possible for every obedience exhibitor to come home a winner (by earning qualifying scores) even though he/she may not earn a placement in the class.

Citilimits I'm Roman, owned by Rosalie Strawcutter, winning Best of Breed at the Woodstock Dog Club.

Most of the obedience titles are awarded after earning three qualifying scores (legs) in the appropriate class under three different judges. These classes offer a perfect score of 200, which is extremely rare. Each of the class exercises has its own point value. A leg is earned after receiving a score of at least 170 and at least 50 percent of the points available in each exercise.

Obedience matches (AKC Sanctioned, Fun, and Show and Go) are usually available. Usually they are sponsored by the local obedience clubs. When preparing an obedience dog for a title, you will find matches very helpful. Fun Matches and Show and Go Matches are more lenient in allowing you to make corrections in the ring. I frequently train (correct) in the ring and inform the judge that I would like to do so and to please mark me "exhibition." This means that I will not be eligible for any prize. This type of training is usually very necessary for the Open and Utility Classes. AKC Sanctioned Obedience Matches do not

At a dog show, you will be asked to gait your dog around the ring according to the judge's instructions.

allow corrections in the ring since they must abide by the AKC Obedience Regulations. If you are interested in showing in obedience, then you should contact the AKC for a copy of the Obedience Regulations.

TRACKING

Tracking is officially classified obedience, but I feel it should have its own category. There are three tracking titles available: Tracking Dog (TD), Tracking Dog Excellent (TDX), Variable Surface Tracking (VST). If all three tracking titles are obtained, then the dog officially becomes a CT (Champion Tracker). The CT will go in front of the dog's name.

A TD may be earned anytime and does not have to follow the other obedience titles. There are many exhibitors that prefer tracking to obedience, and there are others like myself that do both. In my experience with small dogs, I prefer to earn the CD and CDX before attempting tracking. My reasoning is that small dogs are closer to the mat in the

Areas of competition like tracking allow dogs to use their natural abilities, like their fondness of using their noses.

obedience rings and therefore it's too easy to put the nose down and sniff. Tracking encourages sniffing. Of course this depends on the dog. I've had some dogs that tracked around the ring and others (TDXs) who wouldn't think of sniffing in the ring.

Tracking Dog—TD

A dog must be certified by an AKC tracking judge that he is ready to perform in an AKC test. The AKC can provide the names of tracking judges in your area that you can contact for certification. Depending on where you live, you may have to travel a distance if there is no local tracking judge. The certification track will be equivalent to a regular AKC track. A regulation track must be 440 to 500 yards long with at least two right-angle turns out in the open. The track will be aged 30 minutes to two hours. The handler has two starting flags at the beginning of the track to indicate the direction started. The dog works on a harness and 40-foot lead and must work at least 20 feet in front of the handler. An article (either a dark glove or wallet) will be dropped at the end of the track, and the dog must indicate it but not necessarily retrieve it.

People always ask me what the dog tracks. In my opinion, initially, the beginner on the short-aged track tracks the tracklayer. Eventually the dog learns to track the disturbed vegetation and learns to differentiate between tracks. Getting started with tracking requires reading the AKC regulations and a good book on tracking plus finding other tracking enthusiasts. I like to work on the buddy system. That is— we lay tracks for each other so we can practice blind tracks. It is possible to train on your own, but if

This Great Dane is retrieving over the high jump, a required exercise in the Open obedience class.

you are a beginner, it is a lot more entertaining to track with a buddy. Tracking is my favorite dog sport. It's rewarding seeing the dog use his natural ability.

AGILITY

Agility was first introduced by John Varley in England at the Crufts Dog Show, February 1978, but Peter Meanwell, competitor and judge, actually developed the idea. It was officially recognized in the early '80s. Agility is extremely popular in England and Canada and growing in popularity in the U.S. The AKC acknowledged agility in August 1994. Dogs must be at least 12 months of age to be entered. It is a fascinating sport that the dog, handler and spectators enjoy to the utmost. Agility is a spectator sport! The dog performs off lead. The handler either runs with his dog or positions himself on the course and directs his dog with verbal and hand signals over a timed course over or through a variety of obstacles including a time out or pause. One of the main drawbacks to agility is finding a place to train. The obstacles take up a lot of space and it is very time consuming to put up and take down courses.

The titles earned at AKC agility trials are Novice Agility Dog (NAD), Open Agility Dog (OAD), Agility Dog Excellent (ADX), and Master Agility Excellent (MAX). In order to acquire an agility title, a dog must earn a qualifying score in its respective class on three separate occasions under two different judges. The MAX will be awarded after earning ten qualifying scores in the Agility Excellent Class.

Training for performance tests encourages owners to spend more time with their dogs and to retain the natural instincts of the breed.

PERFORMANCE TESTS

During the last decade the American Kennel Club has promoted performance tests—those events that test the different breeds' natural abilities. This type of event encourages a handler to devote even more time to his dog and retain the natural instincts of his breed heritage. It is an important part of the wonderful world of dogs.

Lure Coursing

For all sighthounds (Afghans, Basenjis, Borzois, Greyhounds, Ibizans, Irish Wolfhounds, Pharaoh Hounds, Rhodesian Ridgebacks, Salukis, Scottish Deerhounds, and Whippets).

The participant must be at least one year of age, and dogs with limited registration (ILP) are elgible. They chase a lure of three plastic bags and are judged on overall ability, follow, speed, agility and endurance. Like the other AKC performance tests, lure coursing gives dogs the opportunity to prove themselves at what they were originally bred to do.

Though not a lure-coursing sighthound, your Dane will enjoy opportunities to stretch his legs outdoors.

Junior Courser (JC) A hound running alone shall receive certification from a judge on one date, and a second certification at a later time, stating the hound completed a 600-yard course with a minimum of four turns. The hound must complete the course with enthusiasm and without interruption.

Senior Courser (SC) Must be eligible to enter the open stake and the hound must run with at least one other hound. Must receive qualifying scores at four AKC-licensed or member trials under two different judges.

Field Championship (FC) Prefix to the hound's name. Must receive 15 championship points including two first placements with three points or more under two different judges.

SCHUTZHUND

The German word "Schutzhund" translated to English means "Protection Dog." It is a fast growing competitive sport in the United States and has been popular in England since the early 1900s. Schutzhund was originally a test to determine which German Shepherds were quality dogs for breeding in Germany. It gives us the ability to test our dogs for correct temperament and working ability. Like every other dog sport, it requires teamwork between the handler and the dog.

Schutzhund training and showing involves three phases: Tracking, Obedience and Protection. There are three SchH levels: SchH I (novice), SchH II (intermediate), and SchH III (advanced). Each title becomes progressively more difficult. The handler and dog start out in each phase with 100 points. Points are deducted as errors are incurred. A total perfect score is 300, and for a dog and handler to earn a title he must earn at least 70 points in tracking and obedience and at least 80 points

Great Danes often fare well in Schutzhund competition, going on to win advanced titles.

in protection. Today many different breeds participate successfully in Schutzhund.

General Information

Obedience, tracking and agility allow the purebred dog with an Indefinite Listing Privilege (ILP) number or a limited registration to be exhibited and earn titles. Application must be made to the AKC for an ILP number.

The versatile Great Dane can grow up to participate in many different activities.

The American Kennel Club publishes a monthly *Events* magazine that is part of the *Gazette*, their official journal for the sport of purebred dogs. The *Events* section lists upcoming shows and the secretary or superintendent for them. The majority of the conformation shows in the U.S. are overseen by licensed superintendents. Generally the entry closing date is approximately two-and-a-half weeks before the actual show. Point shows are fairly expensive, while the match shows cost about one third of the point show entry fee. Match shows usually take entries the day of the show but some are pre-entry. The best way to find match show information is through your local kennel club. Upon asking, the AKC can provide you with a list of superintendents, and you can write and ask to be put on their mailing lists.

Obedience trial and tracking test information is available through the AKC. Frequently these events are not superintended, but put on by the host club. Therefore you would make the entry with the event's secretary.

As you have read, there are numerous activities you can share with your dog. Regardless what you do, it does take teamwork. Your dog can only benefit from your attention and training. I hope this chapter has enlightened you and hope, if nothing else, you will attend a show here and there. Perhaps you will start with a puppy kindergarten class, and who knows where it may lead!

Health Care

Veterinary medicine has become far more sophisticated than what was available to our ancestors. This can be attributed to the increase in household pets and consequently the demand for better care for them. Also human medicine has become far more complex. Today diagnostic testing in veterinary medicine parallels human diagnostics. Because of better technology we can expect our pets to live healthier lives thereby increasing their life spans.

Newborn puppies are very vulnerable and need to be checked by a reputable veterinarian within 72 hours of birth.

The First Check Up

You will want to take your new puppy/dog in for its first check up within 48 to 72 hours after acquiring it. Many breeders strongly recommend this check up and so do the humane shelters. A puppy/dog can appear healthy but it may have a serious problem that is not apparent to the layman. Most pets have some type of a minor flaw that may

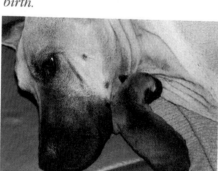

never cause a real problem.

Unfortunately if he/she should have a serious problem, you will want to consider the consequences of keeping the pet and the attachments that will be formed, which may be broken prematurely. Keep in mind there are many healthy dogs looking for good homes.

This first check up is a good time to establish yourself with the veterinarian and learn the office policy regarding their hours and how they handle emergencies. Usually the breeder or another conscientious pet owner is a good reference for

The health of your Great Dane depends on your consistent care and that of a knowledgeable veterinarian.

locating a capable veterinarian. You should be aware that not all veterinarians give the same quality of service. Please do not make your selection on the least expensive clinic, as they may be short changing your pet. There is the possibility that eventually it will cost you more due to improper diagnosis, treatment, etc. If you are selecting a new veterinarian, feel free to ask for a tour of the clinic. You should inquire about making an appointment for a tour since all clinics are working clinics, and therefore may not be available all day for sightseers. You may worry less if you see where your pet will be spending the day if he ever needs to be hospitalized.

THE PHYSICAL EXAM

Your veterinarian will check your pet's overall condition, which includes listening to the heart; checking the respiration; feeling the abdomen, muscles and joints; checking the mouth, which includes the gum color and signs of gum disease along with plaque buildup; checking the ears for signs of an infection or ear mites; examining the eyes; and, last but not least, checking the condition of the skin and coat.

He should ask you questions regarding your pet's eating and elimination habits and invite you to relay your questions. It is a good idea to prepare a list so as not to forget anything. Your veterinarian will likely discuss your puppy's diet with you when you come in for your first check-up. This should have already been provided to you by the breeder. Please keep in mind that not all veterinarians understand the special nutritional needs of a growing Great Dane puppy. Danes should not eat diets that speed growth or keep them too heavy. They should also not need supplements if you are feeding a diet the breeder recommended. Listen to the vet, but ask other Dane breeders for their thoughts, too. It is customary to take in a fresh stool sample (just a small amount) for a test for intestinal parasites. It must be fresh, preferably within 12 hours, since the eggs hatch quickly and after hatching will not be observed under the microscope. If your pet isn't obliging then, usually the technician can take one in the clinic.

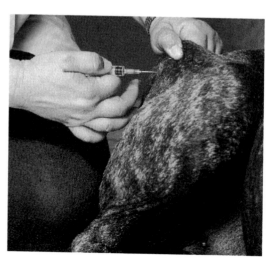

Vaccinations are necessary to protect your dog from potentially life-threatening diseases. Your veterinarian will put your Dane on an immunization schedule.

Great Dane pups have special dietary needs, so before choosing a dog food, follow the advice of both your veterinarian and breeder.

IMMUNIZATIONS

Vaccinations are an important part of a puppy's life. The maternal antibodies begin to fade and lose their effectiveness as the puppy ages. No one knows exactly when this happens in each puppy, which is why a series of vaccinations is usually given from infancy up to 16 weeks of age or so. Because it is expedient, most veterinarians give combination vaccines that may include distemper, hepatitis, leptospirosis, parainfluenza, and parvovirus. There are those who are becoming leery of these mega combinations of vaccines due to adverse reactions and possibly autoimmune problems The puppy needs his vaccines, granted. But it seems much better to separate them somewhat. Ask you vet to give the parvo vaccine separate from the DHLP. Give them a week apart. It's asking an awful lot of the puppy's immune system to develop antibodies to so many viruses at once. *In my opinion,* it's better to be safe than sorry.

There are other vaccines that can be given in addition to the above. I don't give them but I suggest that you discuss them with your vet. Perhaps they're a problem in your area.

Distemper

This is virtually an incurable disease. If the dog recovers, he is subject to severe nervous disorders. The virus attacks every tissue in the body and resembles a bad cold with a fever. It can cause a runny nose and eyes and cause gastrointestinal disorders, including a poor appetite, vomiting and diarrhea. The virus is carried by raccoons, foxes, wolves, mink and other dogs. Unvaccinated youngsters and senior citizens are very susceptible. This is still a common disease.

Your Great Dane will need an annual check-up to maintain good health and minimize any future problems.

Hepatitis

This is a virus that is most serious in very young dogs. It is spread by contact with an infected animal or its stool or urine. The virus affects the liver and kidneys and is characterized by high fever, depression and lack of appetite. Recovered animals may be afflicted with chronic illnesses.

Leptospirosis

This is a bacterial disease transmitted by contact with the urine of an infected dog, rat or other wildlife. It produces severe symptoms of fever, depression, jaundice and internal bleeding and was fatal before the vaccine was developed. Recovered dogs can be carriers, and the disease can be transmitted from dogs to humans.

Parvovirus

This was first noted in the late 1970s and is still a fatal disease. However, with proper vaccinations, early diagnosis and prompt treatment, it is a manageable disease. It attacks the bone marrow and intestinal tract. The symptoms include

Sunnyside Heather is five weeks old. Proper health care from the start will ensure that she will live a long and active life.

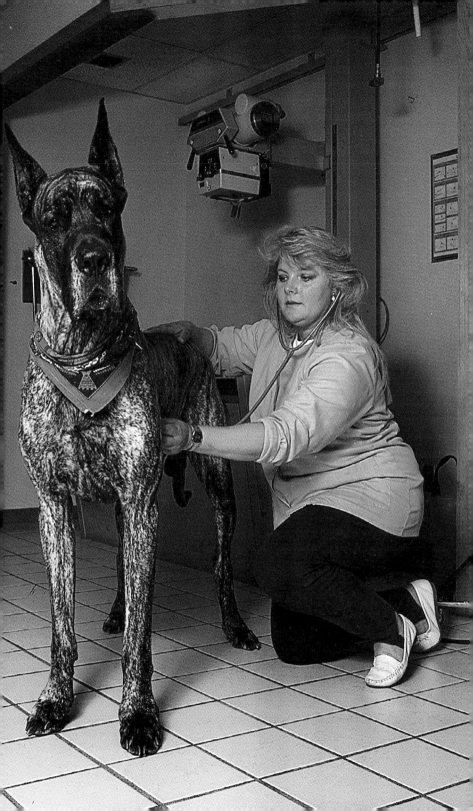

depression, loss of appetite, vomiting, diarrhea and collapse. Immediate medical attention is of the essence.

Rabies

This is shed in the saliva and is carried by raccoons, skunks, foxes, other dogs and cats. It attacks nerve tissue, resulting in paralysis and death. Rabies can be transmitted to people and is virtually always fatal. This disease is reappearing in the suburbs.

Bordetella (Kennel Cough)

The symptoms are coughing, sneezing, hacking and retching accompanied by nasal discharge usually lasting from a few days to several weeks. There are several disease-producing organisms responsible for this disease. The present vaccines are helpful but do not protect for all the strains. It usually is not life threatening but in some instances it can progress to a serious bronchopneumonia. The disease is highly contagious. The vaccination should be given routinely for dogs that come in contact with other dogs, such as through boarding, training class or visits to the groomer.

Coronavirus

This is usually self limiting and not life threatening. It was first noted in the late '70s about a year before parvovirus. The virus produces a yellow/brown stool and there may be depression, vomiting and diarrhea.

Lyme Disease

This was first diagnosed in the United States in 1976 in

Bordetella attached to canine cilia. Otherwise known as kennel cough, this disease is highly contagious and should be vaccinated against routinely.

Lyme, CT in people who lived in close proximity to the deer tick. Symptoms may include acute lameness, fever, swelling of joints and loss of appetite. Your veterinarian can advise you if you live in an endemic area.

The deer tick is the most common carrier of Lyme disease. Photo courtesy of Virbac Laboratories, Inc., Fort Worth, Texas.

After your puppy has completed his puppy vaccinations, you will continue to booster the DHLPP once a year. It is customary to booster the rabies one year after the first vaccine and then, depending on where you live, it should be boostered every year or every three years. This depends on your local laws. The Lyme and corona vaccines are boostered annually and it is recommended that the bordetella be boostered every six to eight months.

ANNUAL VISIT

I would like to impress the importance of the annual check up, which would include the booster vaccinations, check for intestinal parasites and test for heartworm. Today in our very busy world it is rush, rush and see "how much you can get for how little." Unbelievably, some non-veterinary businesses have entered into the vaccination business. More harm than good can come to your dog through improper vaccinations, possibly from inferior vaccines and/or the wrong schedule. More than likely you truly care about your companion dog and over the years you have devoted much time and expense to his well being. Perhaps you are unaware that a vaccination is not just a vaccination. There is more involved. Please, please follow through with regular physical examinations. It is so important for your veterinarian to know your dog and this is especially true during middle age through the geriatric years. More than likely your older dog will require more than one physical a year. The annual physical is good preventive medicine. Through early diagnosis and subsequent treatment your dog can maintain a longer and better quality of life.

Hookworms

These are almost microscopic intestinal worms that can cause anemia and therefore serious problems, including death, in young puppies. Hookworms can be transmitted to humans through penetration of the skin. Puppies may be born with them.

Roundworms

These are spaghetti-like worms that can cause a potbellied appearance and dull coat along with more severe symptoms, such as vomiting, diarrhea and coughing. Puppies acquire these while in the mother's uterus and through lactation. Both hookworms and roundworms may be acquired through ingestion.

Whipworms

These have a three-month life cycle and are not acquired through the dam. They cause intermittent diarrhea usually with mucus. Whipworms are possibly the most difficult worm to eradicate. Their eggs are very resistant to most environmental factors and can last for years until the proper conditions enable them to mature. Whipworms are seldom seen in the stool.

Intestinal parasites are more prevalent in some areas than others. Climate, soil and contamination are big factors contributing to the incidence of intestinal parasites. Eggs are passed in the stool, lay on the ground and then become infective in a certain number of days. Each of the above worms has a different life cycle. Your best chance of becoming and remaining worm-free is to always pooper-scoop your yard. A fenced-in yard keeps stray dogs out, which is certainly helpful.

I would recommend having a fecal examination on your dog twice a year or more often if there is a problem. If your dog has a positive fecal sample, then he will be given the appropriate medication and you will be asked to bring back another stool sample in a certain period of time (depending on the type of worm) and then be rewormed. This process goes on until he has at least two negative samples. The different types of worms require different medications. You will be wasting your money and doing your dog an injustice by buying over-the-counter medication without first consulting your veterinarian.

Coccidiosis and Giardiasis

These protozoal infections usually affect puppies, especially in places where large numbers of puppies are brought together. Older dogs may harbor these infections but do not show signs unless they are stressed. Symptoms include diarrhea, weight loss and lack of appetite. These infections are not always apparent in the fecal examination.

Tapeworms

Seldom apparent on fecal floatation, they are diagnosed frequently as rice-like segments around the dog's anus and the base of the tail. Tapeworms are long, flat and ribbon like, sometimes several feet in length, and made up of many segments about five-eighths of an inch long. The two most common types of tapeworms found in the dog are: (1)First the larval form of the flea tapeworm parasite must mature in an intermediate host, the flea, before it can become infective. Your dog acquires this by ingesting the flea through licking and chewing.

Whipworms can be very hard to find—a task best left to a veterinarian. Pictured here are adult whipworms.

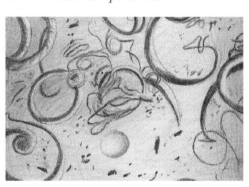

(2) Rabbits, rodents and certain large game animals serve as intermediate hosts for other species of tapeworms. If your dog should eat one of these infected hosts, then he can acquire tapeworms.

HEARTWORM DISEASE

This is a worm that resides in the heart and adjacent blood vessels of the lung that produces microfilaria, which circulate in the bloodstream. It is possible for a dog to be infected with any number of worms from 1 to a 100 that can be 6 to 14 inches long. It is a life-threatening disease, expensive to treat and easily prevented. Depending on where you live, your veterinarian may recommend a preventive year-round and either an annual or semiannual blood test. The most common preventive is given once a month.

EXTERNAL PARASITES

Fleas

These pests are not only the dog's worst enemy but also enemy to the owner's pocketbook. Preventing is less expensive than treating, but regardless I think we'd prefer to spend our money elsewhere. I would guess that the majority of our dogs are allergic to the bite of a flea, and in many cases it only takes one flea bite. The protein in the flea's saliva is the culprit. Allergic dogs have a reaction, which usually results in a "hot spot." More than likely such a reaction will involve a trip to the veterinarian for treatment. Yes, prevention is less expensive. Fortunately today there are several good products available.

If there is a flea infestation, no one product is going to correct the problem. Not only will the dog require treatment, so will the environment. In general, flea collars

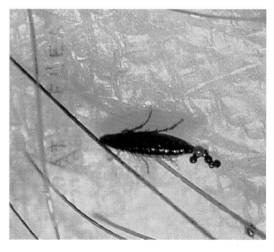

The cat flea is the most common flea of both dogs and cats. Courtesy of Fleabusters, Rx for Fleas, Inc., Fort Lauderdale, Florida.

are not very effective although there is now available an "egg" collar that will kill the eggs on the dog. Dips are the most economical but they are messy. There are some effective shampoos and treatments available through pet shops and veterinarians. An oral tablet arrived on the American market in 1995 and was popular in Europe the previous year. It sterilizes the female flea but will not kill adult fleas. Therefore the tablet, which is given monthly, will decrease the flea population but is not a "cure-all." Those dogs that

Dirofilaria—adult worms in the heart of a dog. Courtesy of Merck Ag Vet.

suffer from flea-bite allergy will still be subjected to the bite of the flea. Another popular parasiticide is permethrin, which is applied to the back of the dog in one or two places depending on the dog's weight. This product works as a repellent causing the flea to get "hot feet" and jump off. Do not confuse this product with some of the organophosphates that are also applied to the dog's back.

Young pups are especially vulnerable to contagious disease, and certain diseases are easily spread from dog to dog. It's very important to keep pups up-to-date in their vaccinations.

Some products are not usable on young puppies. Treating fleas should be done under your veterinarian's guidance. Frequently it is necessary to combine products and the layman does not have the knowledge regarding possible toxicities. It is hard to believe but there are a few dogs that do have a natural resistance to fleas. Nevertheless it would be wise to treat all pets at the same time. Don't forget your cats. Cats just love to prowl the neighborhood and consequently return with unwanted guests.

Adult fleas live on the dog but their eggs drop off the dog into the environment. There they go through four larval stages before reaching adulthood, and thereby are able to jump back on the poor unsuspecting dog. The cycle resumes and takes between 21 to 28 days under ideal conditions. There are environmental products available that will kill both the adult fleas and the larvae.

Your dog's eyes should be checked for any signs of cataracts or infections as part of his regular physical exam.

Ticks

Ticks carry Rocky Mountain Spotted Fever, Lyme disease and can cause tick paralysis. They should be removed with tweezers, trying to pull out the head. The jaws carry disease. There is a tick preventive collar that does an excellent job. The ticks automatically back out on those dogs wearing collars.

Sarcoptic Mange

This is a mite that is difficult to find on skin scrapings. The pinnal reflex is a good indicator of this disease. Rub the ends of the pinna (ear) together and the dog will start scratching with his foot. Sarcoptes are highly contagious to other dogs and to humans although they do not live long on humans. They cause intense itching.

Some breeders will sell their puppies only on the condition that the new owners have the pups spayed or neutered.

Demodectic Mange

This is a mite that is passed from the dam to her puppies. It affects youngsters age three to ten months. Diagnosis is confirmed by skin scraping. Small areas of alopecia around the eyes, lips and/or forelegs become visible. There is little itching unless there is a secondary bacterial infection. Some breeds are afflicted more than others.

Cheyletiella

This causes intense itching and is diagnosed by skin scraping. It lives in the outer layers of the skin of dogs, cats, rabbits and humans. Yellow-gray scales may be found on the back and the rump, top of the head and the nose.

TO BREED OR NOT TO BREED

More than likely your breeder has requested that you have your puppy neutered or spayed. Your breeder's request is based on what is healthiest for your dog and what is most beneficial for your breed. Experienced and conscientious breeders devote many years into developing a bloodline. In order to do this, he makes every effort to plan each breeding in regard to conformation, temperament and health. This type of breeder does his best to perform the necessary testing (i.e., OFA, CERF, testing for inherited blood disorders, thyroid, etc.). Testing is expensive and sometimes very disheartening when a favorite dog doesn't pass his health tests. The health history pertains not only to the breeding stock but to the immediate ancestors. Reputable breeders do not want their offspring to be bred indiscriminately. Therefore you may be asked to neuter or spay your puppy. Of course there is always the exception, and your breeder may agree to let you breed your dog under his direct supervision. This is an important concept. More and more effort is being made to breed healthier dogs.

Spay/Neuter

There are numerous benefits of performing this surgery at six months of age. Unspayed females are subject to mammary and ovarian cancer. In order to prevent mammary cancer she must be spayed prior to her first heat cycle. Later in life, an unspayed female may develop a pyometra (an infected uterus), which is definitely life threatening.

Spaying is performed under a general anesthetic and is easy on the young dog. As you might expect it is a little harder on the older dog, but that is no reason to deny her the surgery. The surgery removes the ovaries and uterus. It is important to remove all the ovarian tissue. If some is left behind, she could remain attractive to males. In order to view the ovaries, a reasonably long incision is necessary. An ovariohysterectomy is considered major surgery.

Neutering the male at a young age will inhibit some characteristic male behavior that owners frown upon. I have found my boys will not hike their legs and mark territory if they are neutered at six months of age. Also neutering at a young age has hormonal benefits, lessening the chance of hormonal aggressiveness.

Surgery involves removing the testicles but leaving the scrotum. If there should be a retained testicle, then he definitely needs to be neutered before the age of two or three years. Retained testicles can develop into cancer. Unneutered males are at risk for testicular cancer, perineal fistulas, perianal tumors and fistulas and prostatic disease.

Intact males and females are prone to housebreaking accidents. Females urinate frequently before, during and after heat cycles, and males tend to mark territory if there is a female in heat. Males may show the same behavior if there is a visiting dog or guests.

Surgery involves a sterile operating procedure equivalent to human surgery. The incision site is shaved, surgically scrubbed and draped. The veterinarian wears a sterile surgical gown, cap, mask and gloves. Anesthesia should be monitored by a registered technician. It is customary for the veterinarian to recommend a pre-anesthetic blood screening, looking for metabolic problems and a ECG rhythm strip to check for normal heart function. Today anesthetics are equal to human anesthetics, which enables your dog to walk out of the clinic the same day as surgery.

Spaying or neutering your puppy will not only control the pet population, but lessens his chances of developing certain health problems later in life.

Some folks worry about their dog gaining weight after being neutered or spayed. This is usually not the case. It is true

that some dogs may be less active so they could develop a problem, but my own dogs are just as active as they were before surgery. I have a hard time keeping weight on them. However, if your dog should begin to gain, then you need to decrease his food and see to it that he gets a little more exercise.

MEDICAL PROBLEMS

Anal Sacs

These are small sacs on either side of the rectum that can cause the dog discomfort when they are full. They should empty when the dog has a bowel movement. Symptoms of inflammation or impaction are excessive licking under the tail and/or a bloody or sticky discharge from the anal area. Breeders like myself recommend emptying the sacs on a regular schedule when bathing the dog. Many veterinarians prefer this isn't done unless there are symptoms. You can express the sacs by squeezing the two sacs (at the five and seven o'clock positions) in and up toward the anus. Take precautions not to get in the way of the foul-smelling fluid that is expressed. Some dogs object to this procedure so it would be wise to have someone hold the head. Scooting is caused by anal-sac irritation and not worms.

Colitis

The stool may be frank blood or blood tinged and is the result of inflammation of the colon. Colitis, sometimes intermittent, can be the result of stress, undiagnosed

It is important that Great Danes used for breeding are screened for all genetic diseases both for the sake of the litter as well as the breed.

whipworms, or perhaps idiopathic (no explainable reason). I have had several dogs prone to this disorder. They felt fine and were willing to eat but would have intermittent bloody stools. If this in an ongoing problem, you should probably feed a diet higher in fiber. Seek professional help if your dog feels poorly and/or the condition persists.

This snoozing puppy is getting the rest he needs to grow big and strong.

The smooth, supple-looking coat and overall condition of Ch. Sunnyside Colorado Columbine radiates good health.

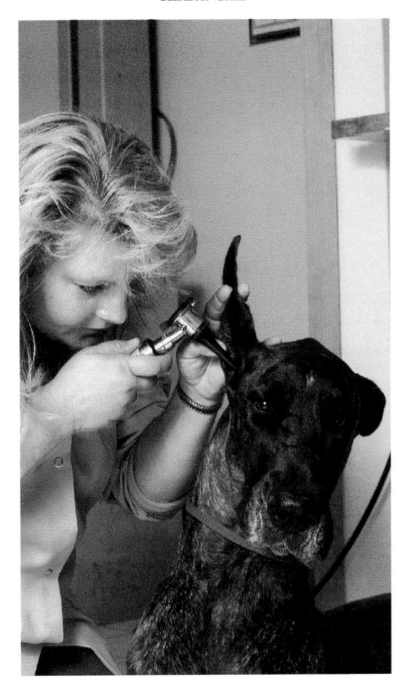

Conjunctivitis

Many breeds are prone to this problem. The conjunctiva is the pink tissue that lines the inner surface of the eyeball except the clear, transparent cornea. Irritating substances such as bacteria, foreign matter or chemicals can cause it to become reddened and swollen. It is important to keep any hair trimmed from around the eyes. Long hair stays damp and aggravates the problem. Keep the eyes cleaned with warm water and wipe away any matter that has accumulated in the corner of the eyes. If the condition persists, you should see your veterinarian. This problem goes hand in hand with keratoconjunctivitis sicca.

Keep your Dane's eyes clear of crusty residue by wiping them with a warm, wet cloth.

Ear Infection

Otitis externa is an inflammation of the external ear canal that begins at the outside opening of the ear and extends inward to the eardrum. Dogs with pendulous ears are prone to this disease, but isn't it interesting that breeds with upright ears also have a high incidence of problems? Allergies, food and inhalent, along with hormonal problems, such as hypothyroidism, are major contributors to the disease. For those dogs which have recurring problems you need to investigate the underlying cause if you hope to cure them.

I recommend that you are careful never to get water into the ears. Water provides a great medium for bacteria to grow. If your dog swims or you inadvertently get water into his ears, then use a drying agent. An at-home preparation would be to use equal parts of three-percent hydrogen peroxide and 70-percent rubbing alcohol. Another preparation is equal parts of white vinegar and water. Your veterinarian alternatively can provide a suitable product. When cleaning the ears, be careful of using cotton tip applicators since they make it easy to pack debris down into the canal. Only clean what you can see.

Dogs with upright ears, such as the Great Dane, are less prone to ear infections, but your vet should still check for waxy build-up or irritation.

If your dog has an ongoing infection, don't be surprised if your veterinarian recommends sedating him and flushing his ears with a bulb syringe. Sometimes this needs to be done a few times to get the ear clean. The ear must be clean so that medication can come in contact with the canal. Be prepared to return for rechecks until the infection is gone. This may involve more flushings if the ears are very bad.

For chronic or recurring cases, your veterinarian may recommend thyroid testing, etc., and a hypoallergenic diet for a trial period of 10 to 12 weeks. Depending on your dog, it may be a good idea to see a dermatologist. Ears shouldn't be taken lightly. If the condition gets out of hand, then surgery may be necessary. Please ask your veterinarian to explain proper ear maintenance for your dog.

Flea Bite Allergy

This is the result of a hypersensitivity to the bite of a flea and its saliva. It only takes one bite to cause the dog to chew or scratch himself raw. Your dog may need medical attention to ease his discomfort. You need to clip the hair around the "hot spot" and wash it with a mild soap and water and you may need to do this daily if the area weeps. Apply an antibiotic anti-inflammatory product. Hot spots can occur from other trauma, such as grooming.

Interdigital Cysts

Check for these on your dog's feet if he shows signs of lameness. They are frequently associated with staph infections and can be quite painful. A home remedy is to soak the infected foot in a solution of a half teaspoon of bleach in a couple of quarts of water. Do this two to three times a day for a couple of days. Check with your veterinarian for an alternative remedy; antibiotics usually work well. If there is a recurring problem, surgery may be required.

Keep your Great Dane happy and healthy by taking him to the veterinarian regularly. He'll thank you for it!

Lameness

It may only be an interdigital cyst or it could be a mat between the toes, especially if your dog licks his feet. Sometimes it is hard to determine which leg is affected. If he is holding up his leg, then you need to see your veterinarian.

Skin

Frequently poor skin is the result of an allergy to fleas, an inhalant allergy or food allergy. These types of problems usually result in a staph dermatitis. Dogs with food allergy usually show signs of severe itching and scratching. However, I have had some dogs with food allergies that never once itched. Their only symptom was swelling of the ears with no ear infection. Food allergy may result in recurrent bacterial skin and ear infections. Your veterinarian or dermatologist will recommend a good restricted diet. It is not wise for you to hit and miss with different dog foods. Many of the diets offered over the counter are not the hypoallergenic diet you are led to believe. Dogs acquire allergies through exposure.

Even a large, hardy dog like the Great Dane can have sensitive skin or allergies. If your dog shows signs of allergic reaction, take him to your veterinarian.

Inhalant allergies result in atopy, which causes licking of the feet, scratching the body and rubbing the muzzle. It may be seasonable. Your veterinarian or dermatologist can perform intradermal testing for inhalant allergies. If your dog should test positive, then a vaccine may be prepared. The results are very satisfying.

Tonsillitis

Usually young dogs have a higher incidence of this problem than the older ones. The older dogs have built up resistance. It is very contagious. Sometimes it is difficult to determine if it is tonsillitis or kennel cough since the symptoms are similar. Symptoms include fever, poor eating, swallowing with difficulty and retching up a white, frothy mucus.

109

DENTAL CARE for Your Dog's Life

So you've got a new puppy! You also have a new set of puppy teeth in your household. Anyone who has ever raised a puppy is abundantly aware of these new teeth. Your puppy will chew anything it can reach, chase your shoelaces, and play "tear the rag" with any piece of clothing it can find. When puppies are newly born, they have no teeth. At about four weeks of age, puppies of most breeds begin to develop their deciduous or baby teeth. They begin eating semi-solid food, fighting and biting with their litter mates, and learning discipline from their mother. As their new teeth come in, they inflict more pain on their mother's breasts, so her feeding sessions become less frequent and shorter. By six or eight weeks, the mother will start growling to warn her pups when they are fighting too roughly or hurting her as they nurse too much with their new teeth.

A thorough oral inspection should be a part of your dog's regular physical exam.

Puppies need to chew. It is a necessary part of their physical and

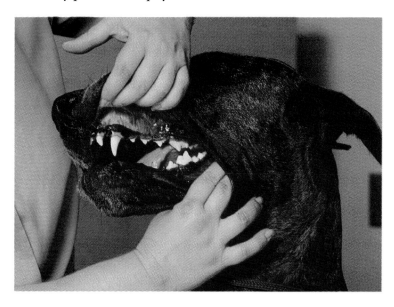

mental development. They develop muscles and necessary life skills as they drag objects around, fight over possession, and vocalize alerts and warnings. Puppies chew on things to explore their world. They are using their sense of taste to determine what is food and what is not. How else can they tell an electrical cord from a lizard? At about four months of age, most puppies begin shedding their baby teeth. Often these teeth need some help to come out and make way for the permanent teeth. The incisors (front teeth) will be replaced first. Then, the adult canine or fang teeth erupt. When the baby tooth is not shed before the permanent tooth comes in, veterinarians call it a retained deciduous tooth. This condition will often cause gum infections by trapping hair and debris between the permanent tooth and the retained baby tooth. Nylafloss® is an excellent device for puppies to use. They can toss it, drag it, and chew on the many surfaces it presents. The baby teeth can catch in the nylon material, aiding in their removal. Puppies that have adequate chew toys will have less destructive behavior, develop more physically, and have less chance of retained deciduous teeth.

Just got a new Great Dane? Give him a dog chew that will promote his well-being: a Nylabone®. It's the only plastic dog bone made of 100% virgin nylon, specially processed to create a tough, durable, completely safe bone. As your Great Dane works a Nylabone®, he's strengthening his teeth and jaws, and he's receiving a gum massage from the tiny bristles that arise as the bone is chewed. Your Dane will enjoy the souper size, available at your local pet shop.

During the first year, your dog should be seen by your veterinarian at regular intervals. Your veterinarian will let you know when to bring in your puppy for vaccinations and parasite examinations. At each visit, your veterinarian should inspect the lips, teeth, and mouth as part of a complete physical examination. You should take some part in the maintenance of your dog's oral health. You should examine your dog's mouth weekly throughout his first year to make sure there are no sores, foreign objects, tooth problems, etc. If your dog drools excessively, shakes its head, or has bad breath, consult your veterinarian. By the time your dog is six months old, the permanent teeth are all in and plaque can start to accumulate on the tooth surfaces. This is when your dog needs to develop good dental-care habits to prevent calculus build-up on its teeth. Brushing is best. That is a fact that cannot be denied. However, some dogs do not like their teeth brushed regularly, or you may not be able to accomplish the task. In that case, you should consider a product that will help prevent plaque and calculus build-up.

The Plaque Attackers® and Galileo Bone® are other excellent choices for the first three years of a dog's life. Their shapes make them interesting for the dog. As the dog chews on them, the solid polyurethane massages the gums which improves the blood circulation to the periodontal tissues. Projections on the chew devices increase the surface and are in contact with the tooth for more efficient cleaning. The unique shape and consistency prevent your dog from exerting excessive force on his own teeth or from breaking off pieces of the bone. If your dog is an aggressive chewer or weighs more than 55 pounds (25 kg), you should consider giving him a Nylabone®, the most durable chew product on the market.

The Gumabone®, made by the Nylabone Company, is constructed of strong polyurethane, which is softer than nylon. Less powerful chewers prefer the Gumabones® to the Nylabones®. A super option for your dog is the Hercules Bone®, a uniquely shaped bone named after the great Olympian for its

exceptional strength. Like all Nylabone products, they are specially scented to make them attractive to your dog. Ask your veterinarian about these bones and he will validate the good doctor's prescription: Nylabones® not only give your dog a good chewing workout but

Puppies will chew just about anything they can get their paws on, so provide your pet with plenty of safe alternatives to things like your furniture.

Your Great Dane will be happier and his teeth and gums healthier if you give him a souper-sized POPpup™ to chew on. Every POPpup™ is 100% edible and enhanced with dog-friendly ingredients like liver, cheese, spinach, carrots or potatoes. What you won't find in a POPpup™ is salt, sugar, alcohol, plastic or preservatives. You can even microwave a POPpup™ to turn it into a huge, crackly treat for your Dane to enjoy.

also help to save your dog's teeth (and even his life, as it protects him from possible fatal periodontal diseases).

By the time dogs are four years old, 75% of them have periodontal disease. It is the most common infection in dogs. Yearly examinations by your veterinarian are essential to maintaining your dog's good health. If your veterinarian detects periodontal disease, he or she may recommend a prophylactic cleaning. To do a thorough cleaning, it will be necessary to put your dog under anesthesia. With modern gas anesthetics and monitoring equipment, the procedure is pretty safe. Your veterinarian will scale the teeth with an ultrasound scaler or hand instrument. This removes the calculus from the teeth. If there are calculus deposits below the gum line, the veterinarian will plane the roots to make them smooth. After all of the calculus has been removed, the teeth are polished with pumice in a polishing cup. If any medical or surgical treatment is needed, it is done at this time. The final step would be fluoride treatment and your follow-up treatment at home. If the periodontal disease is advanced, the veterinarian may prescribe a medicated mouth rinse or antibiotics for use at home. Make sure your dog has safe, clean and attractive chew toys and treats. Chooz® treats are another way of using a consumable treat to help keep your dog's teeth clean.

Rawhide is the most popular of all materials for a dog to chew. This has never been good news to dog owners, because rawhide is inherently very dangerous for dogs. Thousands of dogs have died from rawhide, having swallowed the hide after it has become soft and mushy, only to cause stomach and intestinal blockage. A new rawhide product on the market has finally solved the problem of rawhide: molded Roar-Hide® from Nylabone. These are composed of processed, cut up, and melted American rawhide injected into your dog's favorite shape: a dog bone. These dog-safe devices smell and taste like rawhide but don't break up. The ridges on the bones help to fight tartar build-up on the teeth and they last ten times longer than the usual rawhide chews.

As your dog ages, professional examination and cleaning should become more frequent. The mouth should be inspected at least once a year. Your veterinarian may recommend visits every six months. In the geriatric patient, organs such as the

Why would you want to give your Great Dane a souper-sized CarrotBone™? Because you know carrots are rich in fiber, carbohydrates, and vitamin A. Because it is a durable chew containing no plastics or artificial ingredients of any kind, because it is a 100%-natural plaque, obesity and boredom fighter for your Dane.

Provide your Dane pup with a lot of toys to keep him busy and out of trouble. heart, liver, and kidneys do not function as well as when they were young. Your veterinarian will probably want to test these organs' functions prior to using general anesthesia for dental cleaning. If your dog is a good chewer and you work closely with your veterinarian, your dog can keep all of its teeth all of its life. However, as your dog ages, his sense of smell, sight, and taste will diminish. He may not have the desire to chase, trap or chew his toys. He will also not have the energy to chew for long periods, as arthritis and periodontal disease make chewing painful. This will leave you with more responsibility for keeping his teeth clean and healthy. The dog that would not let you brush his teeth at one year of age, may let you brush his teeth now that he is ten years old.

If you train your dog with good chewing habits as a puppy, he will have healthier teeth throughout his life.

IDENTIFICATION and Finding the Lost Dog

There are several ways of identifying your dog. The old standby is a collar with dog license, rabies, and ID tags. Unfortunately collars have a way of being separated from the dog and tags fall off. I am not suggesting you shouldn't use a collar and tags. If they stay intact and on the dog, they are the quickest way of identification.

For several years owners have been tattooing their dogs. Some tattoos use a number with a registry. Here lies the problem because there are several registries to check. If you wish to tattoo, use your social security number. The humane shelters have the means to trace it. It is usually done on the inside of the rear thigh. The area is first shaved and numbed. There is no pain, although a few dogs do not like the buzzing sound. Occasionally tattooing is not legible and needs to be redone.

The newest method of identification is microchipping. The microchip is a computer chip that is no larger than a grain of rice. The veterinarian implants it by injection between the shoulder blades. The dog feels no discomfort. If your dog is lost and picked up by the humane society, they can trace you by scanning the microchip, which has its own code. Microchip scanners are friendly to other brands of microchips and their registries. The microchip comes with a dog tag saying the

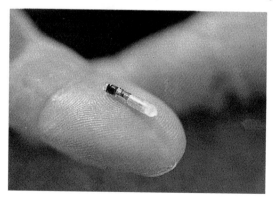

The newest method of identification is microchipping. The microchip is a computer chip that is no bigger than a grain of rice.

dog is microchipped. It is the safest way of identifying your dog.

FINDING THE LOST DOG

I am sure you will agree with me that there would be little worse than losing your dog. Responsible pet owners rarely lose their dogs. They do not let their dogs run free because they don't want harm to come to them. Not only that but in most, if not all, states there is a leash law.

Beware of fenced-in yards. They can be a hazard. Dogs find ways to

Keep close eye on your pet whenever you take him out and about to reduce the chances of becoming separated from each other.

An exercise pen can be helpful in keeping your dog in an enclosed area, but make sure it is large enough to hold your Great Dane.

escape either over or under the fence. Another fast exit is through the gate that perhaps the neighbor's child left unlocked.

Below is a list that hopefully will be of help to you if you need it. Remember don't give up, keep looking. Your dog is worth your efforts.

1. Contact your neighbors and put flyers with a photo on it in their mailboxes. Information you should include would be the dog's name, breed, sex, color, age, source of identification, when your dog was last seen and where, and your name and phone numbers. It may be helpful to say the dog needs medical care. Offer a *reward*.

2. Check all local shelters daily. It is also possible for your dog to be picked up away from home and end up in an out-of-the-way shelter. Check these too. Go in person. It is not good enough to call. Most shelters are limited on the time they can hold dogs then they are put up for adoption or euthanized. There is the possibility that your dog will not make it to the shelter for several days. Your dog could have been wandering or someone may have tried to keep him.

3. Notify all local veterinarians. Call and send flyers.

4. Call your breeder. Frequently breeders are contacted when one of their breed is found.

5. Contact the rescue group for your breed.

6. Contact local schools—children may have seen your dog.

7. Post flyers at the schools, groceries, gas stations, convenience stores, veterinary clinics, groomers and any other place that will allow them.

8. Advertise in the newspaper.

9. Advertise on the radio.

Make sure your dog wears identification tags and a collar at all times. These will be helpful in ensuring his return if he does become lost.

TRAVELING with Your Dog

The earlier you start traveling with your new puppy or dog, the better. He needs to become accustomed to traveling. However, some dogs are nervous riders and become carsick easily. It is helpful if he starts with an empty stomach. Do not despair, as it will go better if you continue taking him with you on short fun rides. How would you feel if every time you rode in the car you stopped at the doctor's for an injection? You would soon dread that nasty car. Older dogs that tend to get carsick may have more of a problem adjusting to traveling. Those dogs that are having a serious problem may benefit from some medication prescribed by the veterinarian.

When traveling with your dog, bring along some things that are familiar to him and that will make him feel at home.

Do give your dog a chance to relieve himself before getting into the car. It is a good idea to be prepared for a clean up with a leash, paper towels, bag and terry cloth towel.

The safest place for your dog is in a fiberglass crate, although close confinement can promote carsickness in some dogs. If your dog is nervous you can try letting him ride on the seat next to you or in someone's lap.

An alternative to the crate would be to use a car harness made for dogs and/or a safety strap attached to the harness or collar. Whatever you do, do not let your dog ride in the back of a pickup truck unless he is securely tied on a very short lead. I've seen trucks stop quickly and, even though the dog was tied, it fell out and was dragged.

I do occasionally let my dogs ride loose with me because I really enjoy their companionship, but in all honesty they

120

If you slowly accustom your Great Dane to car rides, he will start to look forward to coming along!

are safer in their crates. I have a friend whose van rolled in an accident but his dogs, in their fiberglass crates, were not injured nor did they escape. Another advantage of the crate is that it is a safe place to leave him if you need to run into the store. Otherwise you wouldn't be able to leave the windows down. Keep in mind that while many dogs are overly protective in their crates, this may not be enough to deter dognappers. In some states it is against the law to leave a dog in the car unattended.

Never leave a dog loose in the car wearing a collar and leash. I have known more than one dog that has killed himself by hanging. Do not let him put his head out an open window. Foreign debris can be blown into his eyes. When leaving your dog unattended in a car, consider the temperature. It can take less than five minutes to reach temperatures over 100 degrees Fahrenheit.

Crates are a safe way for your dog to travel. The fiberglass crates are safest but the metal crates allow for more air.

TRIPS

Perhaps you are taking a trip. Give consideration to what is best for your dog—traveling with you or boarding. When traveling by car, van or motor home, you need to think ahead about locking your vehicle. In all probability you have many valuables in the car and do not wish to leave it unlocked. Perhaps most valuable and not replaceable is your dog. Give thought to securing your vehicle and providing adequate ventilation for him. Another consideration for you when traveling with your dog is medical problems that may arise and little inconveniences, such as exposure to external parasites. Some areas of the country are quite flea infested. You may want to carry flea spray with you. This is even a good idea when staying in motels. Quite possibly you are not the only occupant of the room.

Unbelievably many motels and even hotels do allow canine guests, even some very first-class ones. Gaines Pet Foods Corporation publishes *Touring With Towser*, a directory of domestic hotels and motels that accommodate guests with dogs. Their address is Gaines TWT, PO Box 5700, Kankakee, IL, 60902. I would recommend you call ahead to any motel that you may be considering and see if they accept pets. Sometimes it is necessary to pay a deposit against room damage. Of course you are more likely to gain accommodations for a small dog than a large dog. Also the management feels reassured when you mention that your dog will be crated. Since my dogs tend to bark when I leave the room, I leave the TV on nearly full blast to deaden the noises outside that tend to encourage my dogs to bark. If you do travel with your dog, take along plenty of baggies so that you can clean up after him. When we all do our share in cleaning up, we make it possible for motels to continue accepting our pets. As a matter of fact, you should practice cleaning up everywhere you take your dog.

Depending on where your are traveling, you may need an up-to-date health certificate issued by your veterinarian. It is good policy to take along your dog's medical information, which would include the name, address and phone number of your veterinarian, vaccination record, rabies certificate, and any medication he is taking.

AIR TRAVEL

When traveling by air, you need to contact the airlines to check their policy. Usually you have to make arrangements up to a couple of weeks in advance for traveling with your dog. The airlines require your dog to travel in an airline

Most Great Danes are happy to accompany their owners on their travels, but always put their comfort and safety first.

approved fiberglass crate. Usually these can be purchased
through the airlines but they are also
readily available in most pet-supply
stores. If your dog is not
accustomed to a crate, then it is a
good idea to get him acclimated to
it before your trip. The day of the
actual trip you should withhold
water about one hour ahead of
departure and no food for about 12
hours. The airlines generally have
temperature restrictions, which do
not allow pets to travel if it is
either too cold or too hot.

Frequently these restrictions are
based on the temperatures at the
departure and arrival airports. It's
best to inquire about a health
certificate. These usually need to
be issued within ten days of
departure. You should arrange for
non-stop, direct flights and if a
commuter plane should be involved,
check to see if it will carry dogs. Some don't. The Humane
Society of the United States has put together a tip sheet for
airline traveling. You can receive a copy by sending a self-
addressed stamped envelope to:

*Your new Great
Dane pup may
have never driven
in a car before. It is
up to you to
pleasantly
introduce him to
traveling.*

    The Humane Society of the United States
    Tip Sheet
    2100 L Street NW
    Washington, DC 20037.

Regulations differ for traveling outside of the country and
are sometimes changed without
notice. Well in advance you need
to write or call the appropriate
consulate or agricultural
department for instructions. Some
countries have lengthy
quarantines (six months), and
countries differ in their rabies
vaccination requirements. For

*Taking along your
Great Dane does not
have to be a hassle if
you plan ahead and
make the necessary
arrangements before
you arrive.*

instance, it may have to be given at least 30 days ahead of your departure.

Do make sure your dog is wearing proper identification. You never know when you might be in an accident and separated from your dog. Or your dog could be frightened and somehow manage to escape and run away. When I travel, my dogs wear collars with engraved nameplates with my name, phone number and city.

Another suggestion would be to carry in-case-of-emergency instructions. These would include the address and phone number of a relative or friend, your veterinarian's name, address and phone number, and your dog's medical information.

BOARDING KENNELS

Perhaps you have decided that you need to board your dog. Your veterinarian can recommend a good boarding facility or possibly a pet sitter that will come to your house. It is customary for the boarding kennel to ask for proof of vaccination for the DHLPP, rabies and bordetella vaccine. The bordetella should have been given within six months of boarding. This is for your protection. If they do not ask for this proof I would not board at their kennel. Ask about flea control. Those dogs that suffer flea-bite allergy can get in trouble at a boarding kennel. Unfortunately boarding kennels are limited on how much they are able to do.

A reputable boarding kennel will require that dogs receive the vaccination for kennel cough no less than two weeks before their scheduled stay.

Be careful about letting your Great Dane put his head out of the window while you are driving. He may get injured or debris may fly into his eyes.

For more information on pet sitting, contact NAPPS:
National Association of Professional Pet Sitters
1200 G Street, NW
Suite 760
Washington, DC 20005.

Our clinic has technicians that pet sit and technicians that board clinic patients in their homes. This may be an alternative for you. Ask your veterinarian if they have an employee that can help you. There is a definite advantage of having a technician care for your dog, especially if your dog is on medication or is a senior citizen.

You can write for a copy of *Traveling With Your Pet* from ASPCA, Education Department, 441 E. 92nd Street, New York, NY 10128.

BEHAVIOR and Canine Communication

Studies of the human/animal bond point out the importance of the unique relationships that exist between people and their pets. Those of us who share our lives with pets understand the special part they play through companionship, service and protection. For many, the pet/owner bond goes beyond simple companionship; pets are often considered members of the family.

Senior citizens show more concern for their own eating habits when they have the responsibility of feeding a dog. Seeing that their dog is routinely exercised encourages the owner to think of schedules that otherwise may seem unimportant to the senior citizen. The older owner may be arthritic and feeling poorly but with responsibility for his dog he has a reason to get up and get moving. It is a big plus if his dog is an attention seeker who will demand such from his owner.

Over the last couple of decades, it has been shown that pets relieve the stress of those who lead busy lives. Owning a pet has been known to lessen the occurrence of heart attack and stroke.

Many single folks thrive on the companionship of a dog. Lifestyles are very different from a long time ago, and today more individuals seek the single life. However, they receive fulfillment from owning a dog.

Most likely the majority of our dogs live in family environments. The companionship they provide is well worth

Children make great playmates for energetic puppies and vice versa!

Dogs are a very important part of their owners' lives. Here, Jill Swedlow poses for a Christmas family portrait with Pepita, Jonquilla, Narcissus and Poppy.

the effort involved. In my opinion, every child should have the opportunity to have a family dog. Dogs teach responsibility through understanding their care, feelings and even respecting their life cycles. Frequently those children who have not been exposed to dogs grow up afraid of dogs, which isn't good. Dogs sense timidity and some will take advantage of the situation.

Today more dogs are serving as service dogs. Since the origination of the Seeing Eye dogs years ago, we now have trained hearing dogs. Also dogs are trained to provide service for the handicapped and are able to perform many different tasks for their owners. Search and Rescue dogs, with their handlers, are sent throughout the world to assist in recovery of disaster victims. They are life savers.

Therapy dogs are very popular with nursing homes, and some hospitals even allow them to visit. The inhabitants truly look forward to their visits. I have taken a couple of my dogs visiting and left in tears when I saw the response of the patients. They wanted and were allowed to have my dogs in their beds to hold and love.

Nationally there is a Pet Awareness Week to educate students and others about the value and basic care of our pets. Many countries take an even greater interest in their pets than Americans do. In those countries the pets are allowed to accompany their owners into restaurants and shops, etc. In the U.S. this freedom is only available to our service dogs. Even so we think very highly of the human/animal bond.

Behavior and health problems can be passed down from generation to generation, so be sure to check your puppy's lineage very carefully.

Canine Behavior

Canine behavior problems are the number-one reason for pet owners to dispose of their dogs, either through new homes, humane shelters or euthanasia. Unfortunately there are too many owners who are unwilling to devote the necessary time to properly train their dogs. On the other hand, there are those who not only are concerned about inherited health problems but are also aware of the dog's mental stability.

You may realize that a breed and his group relatives (i.e., sporting, hounds, etc.) show tendencies to behavioral characteristics. An experienced breeder can acquaint you with his breed's personality. Unfortunately many breeds are labeled with poor temperaments when actually the breed as a whole is not affected but only a small percentage of individuals within the breed.

If the breed in question is very popular, then of course there may be a higher number of unstable dogs. Do not label a breed good or bad. I know of absolutely awful-tempered dogs within one of our most popular, lovable breeds.

Inheritance and environment contribute to the dog's behavior. Some naïve people suggest inbreeding as the cause of bad

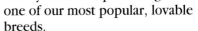

The human/animal bond is a very special one—people thrive on the companionship of their pets. Sunnyside Hillview Starling gives his owner Chris Salyers a big kiss.

temperaments. Inbreeding only results in poor behavior if the ancestors carry the trait. If there are excellent temperaments behind the dogs, then inbreeding will promote good temperaments in the offspring. Did you ever consider that inbreeding is what sets the characteristics of a breed? A purebred dog is the end result of inbreeding. This does not spare the mixed-breed dog from the same problems. Mixed-breed dogs frequently are the offspring of purebred dogs.

When planning a breeding, I like to observe the potential stud and his offspring in the show ring. If I see unruly behavior, I try to look into it further. I want to know if it is genetic or environmental, due to the lack of training and socialization. A good breeder will avoid breeding mentally unsound dogs.

Not too many decades ago most of our dogs led a different lifestyle than what is prevalent today. Usually mom stayed home so the dog had human companionship and someone to discipline it if

Members of the same breed share the same ancestry, and, therefore, many of the same characteristics. However, every dog is an a individual with his own personality.

needed. Not much was expected from the dog. Today's mom works and everyone's life is at a much faster pace.

The dog may have to adjust to being a "weekend" dog. The family is gone all day during the week, and the dog is left to his own devices for entertainment. Some dogs sleep all day waiting for their families to come home and others become wigwam wreckers if given the opportunity. Crates do ensure the safety of the dog and the house. However, he could become physically and emotionally crippled if he doesn't get enough exercise and attention. We still appreciate and want the companionship of our dogs although we expect more from them. In many cases we tend to forget dogs are just that— *dogs,* not human beings.

I own several dogs who are left crated during the day but I do try to make time for them in the evenings and on the weekends. Also we try to do something together before I leave for work. Maybe it helps

Puppies should be socialized with their littermates until they are about 10 weeks old, then separated and introduced to outsiders.

them to have the companionship of other dogs. They accept their crates as their personal "houses" and seem to be content with their routine and thrive on trying their best to please me.

SOCIALIZING AND TRAINING

Many prospective puppy buyers lack experience regarding the proper socialization and training needed to develop the type of pet we all desire. In the first 18 months, training does take some work. Trust me, it is easier to start proper training before there is a problem that needs to be corrected.

The initial work begins with the breeder. The breeder should start socializing the puppy at five to six weeks of age and cannot let up. Human socializing is critical up through 12 weeks of age and likewise important during the following months. The litter should be left together during the first few weeks but it is necessary to separate them by ten weeks of age. Leaving them together after that time will increase competition for litter dominance. If puppies are not socialized with people by 12 weeks of age, they will be timid in later life.

The eight- to ten-week age period is a fearful time for puppies. They need to be handled very gently around children and adults. There should be no harsh discipline during this time. Starting at 14 weeks of age, the puppy begins the juvenile period, which ends when he reaches sexual maturity around six to 14 months of age. During the juvenile period he needs to be introduced to strangers (adults, children and other dogs) on the home property. At sexual maturity he will begin to bark at strangers and become more protective. Males start to lift their legs to urinate but if you desire you can inhibit this behavior by walking your boy on leash away from trees, shrubs, fences, etc.

During your Great Dane's juvenile period, from 14 weeks to 6 months of age, your puppy should meet as many people, children and animals as possible.

Perhaps you are thinking about an older puppy. You need to inquire about the puppy's social experience. If he has lived in a kennel, he may have a hard time adjusting to people and environmental stimuli. Assuming he has had a good social upbringing, there are advantages to an older puppy.

Training includes puppy kindergarten and a minimum of one to two basic training classes. During these classes you will learn how to dominate your youngster. This is especially important if you own a large breed of dog. It is somewhat harder, if not nearly impossible, for some owners to be the Alpha figure when their dog towers over them. You will be taught how to properly restrain your dog. This concept is important. Again it puts you in the Alpha position. All dogs need to be restrained many times during their lives. Believe it or not, some of our worst offenders are the eight-week-old puppies that are brought to our clinic. They need to be gently restrained for a nail trim but the way they carry on you would think we were killing them. In comparison, their vaccination is a "piece of cake." When we ask dogs to do something that is not agreeable to them, then their worst comes out. Life will be easier for your dog if you expose him at a young age to the necessities of life—proper behavior and restraint.

Every dog needs a dominant figure to look to for direction, especially a large breed like the Great Dane. Heather Dillon with Heidi.

Understanding the Dog's Language

Most authorities agree that the dog is a descendent of the wolf. The dog and wolf have similar traits. For instance both are pack oriented and prefer not to be isolated for long periods of time. Another characteristic is that the dog, like the wolf, looks to the leader—Alpha— for direction. Both the wolf and the dog communicate through body language, not only within their pack but with outsiders.

Every pack has an Alpha figure. The dog looks to you, or should look to you, to be that leader. If your dog doesn't receive the proper training and guidance, he very well may replace you as Alpha. This would be a serious problem and is certainly a disservice to your dog.

Eye contact is one way the Alpha wolf keeps order within his pack. You are Alpha so you must establish eye contact with your puppy. Obviously your puppy will have to look at you.

Practice eye contact even if you need to hold his head for five to ten seconds at a time. You can give him a treat as a reward. Make sure your eye contact is gentle and not threatening. Later, if he has been naughty, it is permissible to give him a long, penetrating look. I caution you there are some older dogs that never learned eye contact as puppies and cannot accept eye contact. You should avoid eye contact with these dogs since they feel threatened and will retaliate as such.

The body language of your dog can tell you a lot about his temperament. This Great Dane is bowing to play with her pups.

BODY LANGUAGE

The play bow, when the forequarters are down and the hindquarters are elevated, is an invitation to play. Puppies play fight, which helps them learn the acceptable limits of biting. This is necessary for later in their lives. Nevertheless, an owner may be falsely reassured by the playful nature of his dog's aggression. Playful aggression toward another dog or human may be an indication of serious aggression in the future. Owners should never play fight or play tug-of-war with any dog that is inclined to be dominant.

Signs of submission are:

    1. Avoids eye contact.

    2. Active submission—the dog crouches down, ears back and the tail is lowered.

    3. Passive submission—the dog rolls on his side with his hindlegs in the air and frequently urinates.

Signs of dominance are:

    1. Makes eye contact.

    2. Stands with ears up, tail up and the hair raised on his neck.

    3. Shows dominance over another dog by standing at right angles over it.

Dominant dogs tend to behave in characteristic ways such as:

1. The dog may be unwilling to move from his place (i.e., reluctant to give up the sofa if the owner wants to sit there).
2. He may not part with toys or objects in his mouth and may show possessiveness with his food bowl.
3. He may not respond quickly to commands.
4. He may be disagreeable for grooming and dislikes to be petted.

Dogs are popular because of their sociable nature. Those that have contact with humans during the first 12 weeks of life regard them as a member of their own species—their pack. All dogs have the potential for both dominant and submissive behavior. Only through experience and training do they learn to whom it is appropriate to show which behavior. Not all dogs are concerned with dominance but owners need to be aware of that potential. It is wise for the owner to establish his dominance early on.

Dominant dogs may be unwilling to give up their spot to their owners. These Danes look pretty comfortable on their master's bed.

A human can express dominance or submission toward a dog in the following ways:

1. Meeting the dog's gaze signals dominance. Averting the gaze signals submission. If the dog growls or threatens, averting

Usually, your Great Dane will feel dominant if he stands taller than you, but this puppy looks like he just wants to play!

the gaze is the first avoiding action to take—it may prevent attack. It is important to establish eye contact in the puppy. The older dog that has not been exposed to eye contact may see it as a threat and will not be willing to submit.

2. Being taller than the dog signals dominance; being lower signals submission. This is why, when attempting to make friends with a strange dog or catch the runaway, one should kneel down to his level. Some owners see their dogs become dominant when allowed on the furniture or on the bed. Then he is at the owner's level.

3. An owner can gain dominance by ignoring all the dog's social initiatives. The owner pays attention to the dog only when he obeys a command.

No dog should be allowed to achieve dominant status over any adult or child. Ways of preventing are as follows:

1. Handle the puppy gently, especially during the three- to four-month period.

2. Let the children and adults handfeed him and teach him to take food without lunging or grabbing.

3. Do not allow him to chase children or joggers.
4. Do not allow him to jump on people or mount their legs. Even females may be inclined to mount. It is not only a male habit.
5. Do not allow him to growl for any reason.
6. Don't participate in wrestling or tug-of-war games.
7. Don't physically punish puppies for aggressive behavior. Restrain him from repeating the infraction and teach an alternative behavior. Dogs should earn everything they receive from their owners. This would include sitting to receive petting or treats, sitting before going out the door and sitting to receive the collar and leash. These types of exercises reinforce the owner's dominance.

If your dog seems fearful of people or things, respect his feelings and give him time alone to get used to the situation.

Young children should never be left alone with a dog. It is important that children learn some basic obedience commands so they have some control over the dog. They will gain the respect of their dog.

FEAR

One of the most common problems dogs experience is being fearful. Some dogs are more afraid than others. On the lesser side, which is sometimes humorous to watch, my dog can be afraid of a strange object. He acts silly when something is out of place in the house. I call his problem perceptive intelligence. He realizes the abnormal within his known environment. He does not react the same way in strange environments since he does not know what is normal.

On the more serious side is a fear of people. This can result in backing off, seeking his own space and saying "leave me alone" or it can result in an aggressive behavior that may lead to challenging the person. Respect that the dog wants to be left alone and give him time to come forward. If you approach the cornered dog, he may resort to snapping. If you leave him

The better socialized your Dane is, the less fearful or aggressive he will be.

alone, he may decide to come forward, which should be rewarded with a treat. Years ago we had a dog that behaved in this manner. We coaxed people to stop by the house and make friends with our fearful dog. She learned to take the treats and after weeks of work she overcame her suspicions and made friends more readily.

Some dogs may initially be too fearful to take treats. In these cases it is helpful to make sure the dog hasn't eaten for about 24 hours. Being a little hungry encourages him to accept the treats, especially if they are of the "gourmet" variety. I have a dog that worries about strangers since people seldom stop by my house. Over the years she has learned a cue and jumps up quickly to visit anyone sitting on the sofa. She learned by herself that all guests on the sofa were to be trusted friends. I think she felt more comfortable with them being at her level, rather than towering over her.

Dogs can be afraid of numerous things, including loud noises and thunderstorms. Invariably the owner rewards (by comforting) the dog when it shows signs of fearfulness. I had a terrible problem with my favorite dog in the Utility obedience class. Not only was he intimidated in the class but he was afraid of noise and afraid of displeasing me. Frequently he would knock down the bar jump, which clattered dreadfully. I gave him credit because he continued to try to clear it, although he was terribly scared. I finally learned to "reward" him every time he knocked down the jump. I would jump up and down, clap my hands and tell him how great he was. My psychology worked, he relaxed and eventually cleared the jump with ease. When your dog is frightened, direct his attention to something else and act happy. Don't dwell on his fright.

AGGRESSION

Some different types of aggression are: predatory, defensive, dominance, possessive, protective, fear induced, noise provoked, "rage" syndrome (unprovoked aggression), maternal and aggression directed toward other dogs. Aggression is the most common behavioral problem encountered. Protective breeds are expected to be more aggressive than others but with the proper upbringing they can make very dependable companions. You need to be able to read your dog.

Protective dogs like the Great Dane might tend to show aggression, but with the proper training, they make very dependable pets.

142

Most Danes are incredibly gentle dogs and, when raised and trained correctly, get along with all creatures.

Many factors contribute to aggression including genetics and environment. An improper environment, which may include the living conditions, lack of social life, excessive punishment, being attacked or frightened by an aggressive dog, etc., can all influence a dog's behavior. Even spoiling him and giving too much praise may be detrimental. Isolation and the lack of human contact or exposure to frequent teasing by children or adults also can ruin a good dog.

Lack of direction, fear, or confusion lead to aggression in those dogs that are so inclined. Any obedience exercise, even the sit and down, can direct the dog and overcome fear and/or confusion. Every dog should learn these commands as a youngster, and there should be periodic reinforcement.

When a dog is showing signs of aggression, you should speak calmly (no screaming or hysterics) and firmly give a command that he understands, such as the sit. As soon as your dog obeys, you have assumed your dominant position. Aggression presents a problem because there may be danger to others. Sometimes it is an emotional issue. Owners may consciously or unconsciously encourage their dog's aggression. Other owners show responsibility by accepting the problem and taking measures to keep it under control. The owner is responsible for his dog's actions, and it is not wise to take a chance on someone being bitten, especially a child. Euthanasia is the solution for some owners and in severe cases this may be the best choice. However, few dogs are that dangerous and very few are that much of a threat to their owners. If caution is exercised and professional help is gained early on, then I surmise most cases can be controlled.

Some authorities recommend feeding a lower protein (less than 20 percent) diet. They believe this can aid in reducing aggression. If the dog loses weight, then vegetable oil can be added. Veterinarians and behaviorists are having some success with pharmacology. In many cases treatment is possible and can improve the situation.

If you have done everything according to "the book" regarding training and socializing and are still having a behavior problem, don't procrastinate. It is important that the problem gets attention before it is out of hand.

Dogs love to play tug-of-war, but if your Dane gets aggressive in this game, end it.

This Great Dane's body language tells his owner one thing—let's play!

It is estimated that 20 percent of a veterinarian's time may be devoted to dealing with problems before they become so intolerable that the dog is separated from its home and owner. If your veterinarian isn't able to help, he should refer you to a behaviorist.

PROBLEMS

Barking

This is a habit that shouldn't be encouraged. Over the years I've had new puppy owners call to say that their dog hasn't learned to bark. I assure them they are indeed fortunate but not to worry. Some owners desire their dog to bark so as to be a watchdog. In my experience, most dogs will bark when a stranger comes to the door.

The new puppy frequently barks or whines in the crate in his strange environment and the owner reinforces the puppy's

bad behavior by going to him during the night. This is a no-no. I tell my new owners to smack the top of the crate and say "quiet" in a loud, firm voice. The puppies don't like to hear the loud noise of the crate being banged. If the barking is sleep-interrupting, then the owner should take crate and pup to the bedroom for a few days until the puppy becomes adjusted to his new environment. Otherwise ignore the barking during the night.

Barking can be an inherited problem or a bad habit learned through the environment. It takes dedication to stop the barking. Attention should be paid to the cause of the barking. Does the dog seek attention, does he need to go out, is it feeding time, is it occurring when he is left alone, is it a protective bark, etc.? Presently I have a ten-week-old puppy that is a real loud mouth, which I am sure is an inherited

If you teach your puppy correct behavior, he will always stay as sweet as he looks.

tendency. Both her mother and especially her grandmother are overzealous barkers but fortunately have mellowed with the years. My young puppy is corrected with a firm "no" and gentle shaking and she is responding. When barking presents a problem for you, try to stop it as soon as it begins.

There are electronic collars available that are supposed to curb barking. Personally I have not had experience with them. There are some disadvantages to to the collar. If the dog is barking out of excitement, punishment is not the appropriate treatment. Presumably there is the chance the collar could be activated by other stimuli and thereby punish the dog when it is not barking. Should you decide to use one, then you should seek help from a person with experience with that type of collar. In my opinion I feel the root of the problem needs to be investigated and corrected.

In extreme circumstances (usually when there is a problem with the neighbors), some people have resorted to having their dogs debarked. I caution you that the dog continues to bark but usually only a squeaking sound is heard. Frequently the vocal cords grow

Jumping up can be a sign of affection, but a dog as big as a Great Dane must learn when it is appropriate to do so.

back. Probably the biggest concern is that the dog can be left with scar tissue which can narrow the opening to the trachea.

Jumping Up

Personally, I am not thrilled when other dogs jump on me but I have hurt feelings if they don't! I do encourage my own dogs to jump on me, on command. Some do and some don't. In my opinion, a dog that jumps up is a happy dog. Nevertheless, few guests appreciate dogs jumping on them. Clothes get footprinted and/or snagged.

I am a believer in allowing the puppy to jump up during his first few weeks. In my opinion if you correct him too soon and at the wrong age, you may intimidate him. Consequently he could be timid around humans later in his life. However, there will come a time, probably around four months of age, that he needs to know when it is okay to jump and when he is to show off good manners by sitting instead.

Some authorities never allow jumping. If you are irritated by your dog jumping up on you, then you should discourage it from the beginning. A larger breed of dog can cause harm to a senior citizen. Some are quite fragile. It may not take much to cause a topple that could break a hip.

How do you correct the problem? All family members need to participate in teaching the puppy to sit as soon as he starts to jump up. The sit must be practiced every time he starts to jump up. Don't forget to praise him for his good behavior. If an older dog has acquired the habit, grasp his paws and squeeze tightly. Give a firm "No." He'll soon catch on. Remember the entire family must take part. Each time you allow him to jump up you go back a step in training.

All puppies need to chew; curb destructive chewing by providing your Danes with plenty of toys from Nylabone® to satisfy their urges.

Biting

All puppies bite and try to chew on your fingers, toes, arms, etc. This is the time to teach them to be gentle and not bite hard. Put your fingers in your puppy's mouth and if he bites too hard then say "easy" and let him know he's hurting you. I squeal and act like I have been seriously hurt. If the puppy plays too rough and doesn't respond to your corrections, then he needs "Time Out" in his crate.

A dog the size of a Great Dane needs to be well trained not only for his safety, but for the safety of his owners.

You should be particularly careful with young children and puppies who still have their deciduous (baby) teeth. Those teeth are like needles and can leave little scars on youngsters. My adult daughter still has a small scar on

Garfield shows his social skills and good manners at Amber's birthday party.

Biting should absolutely not be tolerated, and your dog should be taught as a puppy that it is not appropriate behavior.

her face from when she teased an eight-week-old puppy as an eight-year-old.

Biting in the more mature dog is something that should be prevented at all costs. Should it occur I would quickly let him know in no uncertain terms that biting will not be tolerated. When biting is directed toward another dog (dog fight), don't get in the middle of it. On more than one occasion I have had to separate a couple of my dogs and usually was in the middle of that one last lunge by the offender. Some authorities recommend breaking up a fight by elevating the hind legs. This would only be possible if there was a person for each dog. Obviously it would be hard to fight with the hind legs off the ground. A dog bite is serious and should be given attention. Wash the bite with soap and water and contact your doctor. It is important to know the status of the offender's rabies vaccination.

I have several dogs that are sensitive to having mats combed out of their coats and eventually they have had enough. They give fair warning by turning and acting like they would like to nip my offending fingers. However, one verbal warning from me says, "I'm sorry, don't you dare think about biting me and please let me carefully comb just a little bit more." I have owned a minimum of 30 dogs and raised many more puppies and have yet to have one of my dogs bite me except during that last lunge in the two or three dog fights I felt compelled to break up. My dogs

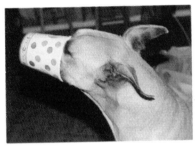

Great Danes love "people food," and Daffodil has gone a little crazy trying to get the last lick of ice cream!

wouldn't dare bite me. They know who is boss.

This is not always the case for other owners. I do not wish to frighten you but when biting occurs you should seek professional help at once. On the other hand you must not let your dog intimidate you and be so afraid of a bite that you can't discipline him. Professional help through your veterinarian, dog trainer and/or behaviorist can give you guidance.

Digging

Bored dogs release their frustrations through mischievous behavior such as digging. For the life of me I do not understand why people own dogs only to keep them outside. Dogs shouldn't be left unattended outside, even if they are in a fenced-in yard. Usually the dog is sent to "jail" (the backyard) because the owner can't tolerate him in the house. The culprit feels socially deprived and needs to be included in the owner's life. The owner has neglected the dog's training. The dog has not developed into the companion we desire. If you are one of these owners, then perhaps it is possible for you to change. Give him another chance. Some owners object to their dog's unkempt coat and doggy odor. See that he is groomed on a regular schedule and look into some training classes.

Submissive Urination

If you supervise your Great Dane and keep him on his lead when outside, running away should not be a problem.

This is not a housebreaking problem. It can occur in all breeds and may be more prevalent in some breeds. Usually it occurs in puppies but occasionally it occurs in older dogs and may be in response to physical praise. Try verbal praise or ignoring your dog until after he has had a chance to relieve himself. Scolding will only make the problem worse. Many dogs outgrow this problem.

Coprophagia

Also know as stool eating, sometimes occurs without a cause. It may begin with boredom and then becomes a habit that is hard to break. Your best remedy is to keep the puppy on a leash and keep the yard picked up. Then he won't have an opportunity to get in trouble. I do not like to clean up accidents or "poop scoop" the yard in front of puppies. I'm suspicious that some puppies try to help and will clean up the stool before I have a chance. Your veterinarian can dispense a medication that is put on the dog's food that makes the stool taste bitter. Of course this will do little good if your dog cleans up after other dogs.

The Runaway

There is little excuse for a dog to run away since dogs should never be off leash except when supervised in the fenced-in yard.

Boredom is one of the leading causes of problem behavior, so make sure your Danes participate in activities and exercise regularly.

I receive phone calls on a regular basis from prospective owners that want to purchase a female since a male is inclined to roam. It is true that an intact male is inclined to roam, which is one of the reasons a male should be neutered. However, females will roam also, especially if they are in heat. Regardless, these dogs should never be given this opportunity. A few years ago one of our clients elected euthanasia for her elderly dog that radiographically appeared to have an intestinal blockage. The veterinarian suggested it might be a corncob. She assured him that was not possible since they hadn't had any. Apparently he roamed and raided the neighbor's garbage and you guessed it—he had a corncob blocking his intestines. Another dog raided the neighbor's garbage and died from toxins from the garbage.

To give the benefit of the doubt, perhaps your dog escapes or perhaps you are playing with your dog in the yard and he refuses to come when called. You now have a runaway. I have had this happen on a smaller scale in the house and have, even to my embarrassment, witnessed this in the obedience ring. Help! The first thing to

They may look harmless and sweet, but you will not believe the mischief that these puppies may get into when a few weeks older!

If your dog does run away while playing with you, do not scold him when he returns. He'll be less likely to want to come to you when called.

remember is when you finally do catch your naughty dog, you must not discipline him. The reasoning behind this is that it is quite possible there could be a repeat performance, and it would be nice if the next time he would respond to your sweet command.

Always kneel down when trying to catch the runaway. Dogs are afraid of people standing over them. Also it would be helpful to have a treat or a favorite toy to help entice him to your side. After that initial runaway experience, start practicing the recall with your dog. You can let him drag a long line (clothesline) and randomly call him and then reel him in. Let him touch you first. Reaching for the dog can frighten him. Each time he comes you reward him with a treat and eventually he should get the idea that this is a nice experience. The long line prevents him from really getting out of hand. My dogs tend to come promptly within about 3 to 4 feet (out of reach) and then turn tail and run. It's "catch me if you can." At least with the long line you can step on it and stop him.

Food Guarding

If you see signs of your puppy guarding his food, then you should take immediate steps to correct the problem. It is not fair to your puppy to feed him in a busy environment where children or other pets may interfere with his eating. This can be the cause of food guarding. I always recommend that my puppies be fed in their crates where they do not feel threatened. Another advantage of this is that the puppy gets down to the business of eating and doesn't fool around. Perhaps you have seen possessiveness over the food bowl or his toys. Start by feeding him out of your hand and teach him that it is okay for you to remove his food bowl or toy and that you most assuredly will return it to him. If your dog is truly a bad actor and intimidates you, try keeping him on leash and perhaps sit next to him making happy talk. At feeding time make him work for his reward (his dinner) by doing some obedience command such as sit or down. Before your problem gets out of control you should get professional help. If he is out of control over toys, perhaps you should dispose of them or at least put them away when young children are around.

All puppies may experience some behavioral problems, but most will outgrow them in time.

Mischief and Misbehavior

All puppies and even some adult dogs will get into mischief at some time in their lives. You should start by "puppy proofing" your house. Even so it is impossible to have a sterile environment. For instance, if you would be down to four walls and a floor your dog could still chew a hole in the wall. What do you do? Remember puppies should never be left unsupervised so let us go on to the trusted adult dog that has misbehaved. His behavior may be an attention getter. Dogs, and even children, are known to do mischief even though they know they will be punished. Your puppy/dog will benefit from more attention and new direction. He may benefit from a

Great Danes are versatile, intelligent and loving animals that make wonderful pets. This is Ch. Sunnyside Skylark V. Raseac, owned by the author and Brucie Mitchell.

training class or by reinforcing the obedience he has already learned. How about a daily walk? That could be a good outlet for your dog, time together and exercise for both of you.

Separation Anxiety

This occurs when dogs feel distress or apprehension when separated from their owners. One of the mistakes owners make is to set their dogs up for their departure. Some authorities recommend paying little attention to the pet for at least ten minutes before leaving and for the first ten minutes after you arrive home. The dog isn't cued to the fact you are leaving and if you keep it lowkey they learn to accept it as a normal everyday occurrence. Those dogs that are used to being crated usually accept your departure. Dogs that are anxious may have a serious problem and wreak havoc on the house within a few minutes after your departure. You can try to acclimate your dog to the separation by leaving for just a few minutes at a time, returning and rewarding him with a treat. Don't get too carried away. Plan on this process taking a long time. A behaviorist can set down a schedule for you. Those dogs that are insecure, such as ones obtained from a humane shelter or those that have changed homes, present more of a problem.

Punishment

A puppy should learn that correction is sometimes necessary and should not question your authority. An older dog that has never received correction may retaliate. In my opinion there will be a time for physical punishment but this does not mean hitting the dog. Do not use newspapers, fly swatters, etc. One type of correction, that is used by the mother dog when she corrects her puppies, is to take the puppy by the scruff and shake him *gently*. For the older, larger dog you can grab the scruff, one hand on each side of his neck, and lift his legs off the ground. This is effective since dogs feel intimidated when their feet are off the ground. Timing is of the utmost importance when punishment is necessary. Depending on the degree of fault, you might want to reinforce punishment by ignoring your dog for 15 to 20 minutes. Whatever you do, do not overdo corrections or they will lose value.

My most important advice to you is to be aware of your dog's actions. Even so, remember dogs are dogs and will behave as such even though we might like them to be perfect little people. You and your dog will become neurotic if you worry about every little indiscretion. When there is reason for concern—don't waste time. Seek guidance. Dogs are meant to be loved and enjoyed.

References:

Manual of Canine Behavior, Valerie O'Farrell, British Small Animal Veterinary Association.

Good Owners, Great Dogs, Brian Kilcommons, Warner Books.

SUGGESTED READING

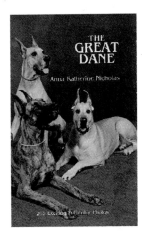

PS-826
The Great Dane

TS-258
Training your Dog for Sports and other Activities
160 pages, over 200 full-color photos.

TS-249
Skin and Coat Care for your Dog
224 pages, over 190 full-color photos.

TS-214
Owner's Guide to Dog Health
432 pages, over 300 photos.

INDEX